Endorsement

CW00519460

I love hearing stories of transformation, especially when it is clear that Jesus is the hero! That's powerfully the case here. May reading Glenn's story point many to Jesus, who alone can bring hope in their darkest nights and peace in their most troubled moments.

Paul Harcourt
Ambassador for New Wine England

Colossians 1:13 says, " He has delivered us from the domain of darkness and transferred us to the kingdom of his beloved Son." Glenn's story is about how dark that domain can be and how far you can be from knowing God's mercy and grace. It's also the story of how God can deliver you. No darkness is too dark for the light of God to penetrate. It's the story of the life-transforming gospel that is available to all of us.

David Holden
Leader of the New Ground family of churches
(part of Newfrontiers)

From the first moment Glenn shared part of his story with me years ago, I always knew it would make for riveting reading. And this book does not disappoint. The Bible tells us that we overcome Satan by the blood of the Lamb (Jesus) and the word of our testimony (Rev.12:11). My prayer is that as people read this, hell will be plundered and heaven populated. Glenn's stories are testaments of God's faithfulness and signposts for anyone feeling lost or trapped in darkness and confusion. Once you've read it, please pass it on to someone else who needs it.

Chip Kendall
Soul Children UK

This is a most remarkable supernatural story of redemption and reconciliation; it's good overcoming evil, light over darkness. The writing style may be rough and ready, but the God story is sublime. Glenn's account of triumph in the face of adversity and hardship will give hope to anyone who finds themselves at the sharp end of life. How does an ex-drug user and drinker from a fractured family on a difficult council estate end up pastoring a church in the salubrious surroundings of Sevenoaks? Answer: he totally and continually surrenders his life to God. Glenn's complete trust in God for both provision and power is breathtaking. I love his boldness and unswerving obedience as he follows God's path regardless of the consequences. What an adventure!

Paul Brown

Minister, City Hope Church, London
Co-author of *Invisible Divides: Class, culture and barriers to belonging in the Church*

From the first paragraph of this gripping and gritty testimony, Glenn is extremely open about his real-life experiences and struggles. Here is the true story of how only Jesus can transform any life, no matter who that individual is or what they have experienced. So refreshing to read such an honest account of one man's struggle with life on his journey both to faith in and with Jesus since. A good response to Psalm 105:1: "Give praise to the Lord, proclaim his name; make known among the nations what he has done."

Pastor James Bell

Community Chaplain, Edge Ministries

This is a raw, honest and authentic memoir of a broken life transformed by an encounter with a loving, powerful God. Glenn narrates his journey from addiction, crime and witchcraft to freedom and healing in Jesus.

Matt Partridge

Core Team and Eldership Team Leader
Emmanuel Church, Oxford

"How can God hear a man like you?"

From drugs, occult and violence to freedom, hope and peace

GLENN WALSH

O&U
Onwards & Upwards

Onwards and Upwards Publishers

4 The Old Smithy
London Road
Rockbeare
EX5 2EA
United Kingdom
www.onwardsandupwards.org

Copyright © Glenn Walsh 2023

The right of Glenn Walsh to be identified as the author of this work has been asserted by the author in accordance with the Copyright, Designs and Patents Act 1988.

All rights reserved.

No part of this publication may be reproduced or transmitted in any form or by any means, electronic or mechanical, including photocopy, recording or any information storage and retrieval system, without permission in writing from the author or publisher.

First edition, published in the United Kingdom by Onwards and Upwards Publishers Ltd. (2023).

ISBN: 978-1-78815-947-0
Typeface: Sabon LT

Some names and identifying details have been changed to protect the privacy of individuals.

Unless otherwise indicated, Scripture quotations are taken from the Holy Bible, New International Version® Anglicized, NIV®. Copyright © 1979, 1984, 2011 by Biblica, Inc.® Used by permission. All rights reserved worldwide.

Scripture quotations marked (NKJV) are taken from the New King James Version®. Copyright © 1982 by Thomas Nelson. Used by permission. All rights reserved.

About the Author

Glenn Walsh is the pastor at Vine Evangelical Church in Kent. He and his wife Sarah have a background of church planting, mission and youth work, serving with the Newfrontiers, Vineyard and New Wine expressions of churches. Glenn and Sarah have six daughters, twelve grandchildren (at present) and have been foster carers to over 30 babies and children. Glenn had a dramatic conversion in his early twenties with God moving sovereignly in life; his story has featured in national publications and evangelistic recordings, and he has shared his story over the years in many settings, including prisons, radio, churches and schools.

To contact the author, please write to:

Glenn Walsh
c/o Onwards and Upwards Publishers
4 The Old Smithy
London Road
Rockbeare
EX5 2EA

Contents

"How Can God Hear A Man Like You?"

Prologue

Seemingly out of nowhere I heard an audible voice speak to me: "If you pray with iniquity in your heart, your prayers are in vain." I recognised the words as a quote from the Bible[1] and considered the battle going on in my heart.

I was fighting against all kinds of desires; evil thoughts constantly raged through my mind, shouting, demanding my attention.

"Look at you! How can God hear a man like you? Your heart is corrupt and full of evil; God does not hear you! All your prayers are in vain!"

I knew the assessment was right. I couldn't fight any more; if the one I sought could not even look on me, then I was lost and I knew I deserved the punishment that was coming. The final scraps of fight in me trickled away. I seemed to lose the grip on the hand of hope that I had tried so hard to hold on to. I felt truly alone, peering into eternity. *Then it's true, I'm destined for hell. I can't go through all this and end up there anyway, so I may as well go tonight.*

Grabbing a knife from my bedroom drawers I set off downstairs.

"What's wrong with you? Look at your face; it's covered in blotches!" my concerned mother said as I entered the living room.

I glanced into a mirror and saw a pale face covered in huge purple circles staring emptily back.

"I just need some fresh air," I answered her. I couldn't let my own mother near my turmoil; I had to protect her and everyone else near to me.

I ended up in the same field where the battle had started so many months ago. I placed my hand in my pocket and thumbed the knife. *This is not a cry for help, for there is no one who can help me; my only hope is gone. I know some will grieve for me, saying, "A wasted young life of only twenty-one years; he had so much to live for. If only we knew..." But as long as I remain alive, not one of them is safe.*

I was so afraid, so alone, truly lost.

---

[1] Psalm 66:18

To end up in hell just seemed a slight transition from life to death, as I dwelt there anyway.

There was no light at the end of this tunnel; I would live in torment by day and night, deprived of peace and sleep, only to find it was all just wasted hope.

Making sure I was truly alone in the darkness – just wanting to end it all while retaining the knowledge that death was not the end – and not wanting to be found, I glanced around. I then noticed a light shining from the nearby building to my right, so I went over to peer through a window, just to make double sure that I was alone. I had failed enough in this life already so a botched ending was the last thing I wanted.

Through the window of this closed school building I could see a spotlight which was illuminating a poster that had been positioned on a tripod; it was standing in the corner of an empty hall. I stood there in disbelief. *Who placed it there? This isn't a church or a religious building! Why did they leave a light shining?* As I read the words on the poster, they penetrated my very soul.

"And surely I am with you always, to the very end of the age."[2]

The accusing voice was instantly silenced. My upside-down world turned the right way round; the "valley of the shadow of death" that I had walked through suddenly – *instantly* – changed, and I now was standing on a solid, firm, stable foundation that could not be shaken. Once again I could now face the battle afresh. A living hope had been restored to me in an instant.

The voice of the accuser had led me to this place to have me end it all – or so I had thought. Now, instead, I recognised that the voice of the Good Shepherd had been calling me there all along, to bring me to a new knowledge of his overshadowing goodness. Instead of death and destruction, I stumbled on life and refreshed hope.

Once more, this Jesus whom I was fighting to know had exploded into my reality, bringing light and hope into my confused and desperate world. How meaningful Psalm 23:4 was to me that night: "Even though I walk through the darkest valley, I will fear no evil, for you are with me; your rod and your staff, they comfort me."

It had taken me about a year to get to this point since I had experienced a certain dreadful night of hopelessness and darkness. Now these had been replaced with an experience of foundational faith. Just as

---

[2] Matthew 28:20

4

on that dreadful night, I had found that when I was utterly lost, he was there for me.

CHAPTER ONE

That Dreadful Night

That Sunday night started as many others had: what drugs were at hand, what could I score, who was around? As usual I found myself in the company of Cybele. She'd become my closest friend over the past couple of years. Although I had a deep hatred of her, I was also drawn to her; thoughts of her dominated my mind day and night. At one time I had literally put a huge distance between us of nearly two hundred miles, but she had still ended up on my doorstep and once again become the central focus of my life. Try as I could, I just couldn't shake off this bittersweet relationship.

Nearing the end of a usual binge of cannabis, Cybele said, "Got some 'acid'. Want one?"

"Silly question!" I answered.

Cybele and I both dropped a blotter with a superman print on it and went for a walk. Unlike all the other LSD trips that I had experienced, the unfolding of this night's events would change my life forever, the details etched in my mind driving me from a living insanity to a search for peace.

The effects of LSD could take up to an hour to manifest in me from the time of dropping a tab, but I could feel this one take hold of me almost instantly.

As we walked out of her flat and through the estate, I passed an old girlfriend who was walking with a former acquaintance of mine who disliked me intently. Both Cybele and I laughed as we walked past them, intending to provoke a response, but they just scurried on.

We headed towards the town centre and met up with a few others. The conversations tended to dwell on the things we'd all got up to, stories that amused us and showed how 'bad' we were.

"Let's walk," Cybele called over to me. We said our goodbyes to the others and walked towards the west of town. As we trod along the streets, we reminisced on the adventures we'd had, our time in Dorset living in a field, the parties, our time of being handcuffed together and being led away by armed police.

Suddenly I stopped and said, "I can feel the power coming." I raised my arms outwards to experience a wave of what felt like external power moving on me. I often felt this either through occult practice or under the influence of drugs, especially LSD.

"No, not tonight!" Cybele commanded.

Instantly the feeling stopped and I was brought back to a sober-like state, although still clearly not in my right mind.

Cybele then guided the conversation as we continued on a road of remembrance of all the paranormal experiences we'd had through our dabbling with the occult.

"Let's go to the spiritualist church. After all, that medium did say you'd go back," Cybele laughed.

"Blimey, don't remind me! You must be kidding!" I answered.

Reluctantly, though, I followed as she led the way towards the spiritualist church building, all the time remembering the panic I had felt throughout the whole service and how that woman had pinpointed me out of the crowd. I laughed as I remembered her inaccuracy over what she thought was a dead relative of mine, although her message to me had been disturbingly relevant.

As we neared the building, the whole road, although moonlit, was dark and shadowy; fortunately there were no services on so the building was closed.

We stood on the drive looking towards the building. A presence of deep heavy darkness emanated from it like a spiritually induced fog; squinting through the darkness I could almost make out a shadow-like figure lurking in the darkness of the drive. Then Cybele once again broke my chain of thoughts as she spontaneously began to run up the road laughing.

I caught up with her and we stood together laughing for a good five minutes.

"Did you see that shadow figure?" she asked.

"Shut up! Did we both see that? Blimey, we're a bit stupid playing with this stuff while we're tripping," I answered

Cybele laughed again and walked towards the old school field, while I was filled with a distinct uneasiness and strong feelings of apprehension. I followed her, pushing those feelings away.

As we entered the moonlit open expanse of the field, Cybele turned to me and asked, "What are you afraid of? What are you holding on to? Why are you so afraid to lose yourself? I will have you, Glenn; I will have you." She laughed for a while, then stopped and looked at me intently. Pointing directly at my heart, she said coldly, "Satan wants you!"

An overwhelming sudden panic engulfed me. Instantly my mind began to conjure up images of newspaper headlines like one I had read recently: "Man kills close ones through drug induced frenzy". But I could see *my* name on the front cover.

Cybele was spinning and laughing as turmoil filled my mind. I had suffered panic attacks for as long as I could remember, but through the maze of confusion I could find no way out of this one. Finally I had gone too far; my life literally flashed before my eyes, as did what I perceived as my future. I could see great evil being done at my own hands. A force gripped my soul to bend it, to snuff out any moral goodness that may have been left in me; blackest darkness consumed my whole being. I had had many LSD trips, but none like this. I tried all I could to resist the murderous thoughts that raged through my mind. Cybele just laughed on and on, spinning and dancing. Then I felt myself leave my body. Suddenly I was looking down on the earth, powerless, lost, defeated. "You will do my bidding," a stern voice commanded.

From this place of utter hopelessness and darkness, I cried out from the chasm of my soul – a cry, a plea, in the direction that contradicted all that I was: "God, if you're real, if you can, *help me!*"

Immediately I found myself standing in the field again, watching Cybele dancing and spinning. But then, again, the darkness engulfed me. I felt my entire being, all that I understood as 'me', my identity and self-awareness, just slip away through my fingers. Inside my mind, from my ebbing soul, the last part of me that felt it was about to die, I cried out in pure desperation once again: "*God, help me! Save me, please!*"

Lost... Deepest darkness... A screaming void of fear...

Then suddenly a new voice spoke into this desperation, a small whisper that cut through the darkness: "Everyone who calls on the name of the Lord will be saved."

Instantly Cybele stopped her gyrating. Holding her head in her hands, she begun to scream.

"Everyone who calls on the name of the Lord will be saved." This revelation echoed through my mind, as Cybele grew hysterical, screaming out in a violent rage, "NO, NO, NO!"

The stern voice returned to my mind: "How can you call on God? You are a chief blasphemer; look at all the evil you've done! Remember all those things you said? You are mine!"

But louder still, "Everyone who calls on the name of the Lord will be saved," resounded through my thoughts, refuting the accusations.

"Look at my power, the things you have seen and done. Just think it and they will die!" the stern voice mocked as faces of loved ones flashed before me.

No, I will be saved; it's going to be OK, I tried to reassure myself.

All the while my assurance was challenged to its foundations. I was a chronic blasphemer, full of hate and evil desires; how could I even call on God or expect him to help me? I was a self-confessed God-hater – and yet... everyone, yes, *everyone* who calls on the name of the Lord will be saved. This voice of hope spoke louder still. I didn't understand it, I didn't know how it was possible, but somehow I knew I was going to be saved.

I ran over to the still-screaming Cybele. Grabbing her by her shoulders, I snapped her out of her hysterical state. She turned and ran toward the exit and I followed closely behind.

As we entered the street-lighted road she turned to me and said, "Welcome to the horrors..."

"STOP!" I commanded her.

We stood there in silence for a while, then headed back to my house. I just wanted to fall asleep, to make this nightmare stop, to change the whole subject. We ended up in my bedroom for the night, but sleep evaded us for most of it. Instead, distorted childhood memories and terrifying thoughts flooded in and out of my mind. I could not see any way forward or any way out of this self-destructive nightmare of a life that I had navigated myself into. "Just think it and they will die. You will do my bidding; you are mine." It felt like tormenting.

A battle raged within me as powerful entities tried to take over my will again and again, then my fears increased as my thoughts turned from myself to those around me.

It's the 'acid'; it's just a bad trip. All this will pass. It's the 'acid'. It'll go away; I just have to sleep, I repeated to myself again and again.

Eventually both sleep then morning came.

After we heard the door shut and felt sure my mother had left the house, Cybele and I got ourselves ready, both still shellshocked like a couple of refugees emerging from the rubble and destruction of a war-torn village.

"Coming round mine?" Cybele enquired.

"Later... Just trying to get my head together," I answered.

Cybele left and I was alone. I wandered about the house trying to make sense of the previous night. Was any of it real? Was it just a bad trip, "the horrors" as I'd heard them described so many times? What of the reality of the spiritual experiences I had had during recent years; was I playing with fire and had finally got burned?

I sat for hours trying to make sense of all this, but without success. "I will have you, Glenn! You are mine!" Once again I felt myself being taken over by a force that threatened to drive me right back into that field experience.

"No, no! God, help me! I won't go back there. God, help me! Save me from myself and I'll do whatever you ask of me!" I pleaded.

"Just look at you," my thoughts echoed. "You're the one who boasted before men that God was dead. You're the one who stood and asked God to strike you down dead if he had any power, and boasted mockingly to the ones who believe in him. Now you call on him and expect him to answer?" Doubts of God's help filled my mind, but somehow I began to cling to what I knew I had heard, just as a single drop of rain in a drought-filled land brings hope of life: *Everyone who calls on the name of the Lord will be saved.*

I seriously doubted that this small thought would be enough though to get me through the onslaught of evil that was gripping my mind and even my body. I could feel waves pass through me, a compressing feeling in my arms, running down my legs, drowning out my natural senses.

Would I ever be the same again? I was surely and completely lost, but maybe, *just maybe,* there was a God that would save me.

CHAPTER TWO

The Sign

Eventually, later that morning, I got my head together enough to go round to Cybele's. On my arrival she seemed to be in a pretty good mood; a few other friends were there, all smoking spliffs.

"Talk about the horrors!" Cybele laughed.

"Worst night ever!" I answered, but I didn't feel like talking much. "Still coming down... Pass me a joint?" I asked.

I sat there smoking in silence and picked up a book to read. I found one of many on the occult and started browsing through the book, looking for any chapter that might help give me a bit of peace in my mind. I was familiar with most of what the book offered, but one chapter grabbed my attention. Walking with the gods, the turmoil and battles, and the fear of fear itself were subtitled throughout this particular chapter. It took me from merely dabbling with the occult through to the cult of Satan worship! *Boom!* I had finally woken up. Cybele glanced my way and chuckled. Pictures of satanic rituals were there in front of me. This was no game that I'd been playing; this was real.

Cybele had told me many times of a satanic priest and priestess that had initiated her into a cult and how they had wanted to meet me, that she was recruiting me for them. Somehow, though, I had thought it all a weird game. *What the hell have I been playing with?*

I remembered how I had torn the old family Bible and cursed God with my mouth when I had only been about eight years old. Over the years I had taken communion with 'acid', communicated with spirits and had so many weird experiences – and I had hated those Bible-bashers. Now it all became so clear: I was anti-God, anti-Christ, and therefore the devil's own and destined for hell. I had done so many evil things, hurt so many people just to please myself.

I couldn't stay in this company; I had to go somewhere – but where? I couldn't go home because I was growing more afraid to be alone with anyone, afraid for their safety.

Without any explanation I just rose to my feet and exited Cybele's flat. Once outside I just walked and walked, confused, scared, not knowing where to go or who could help me. I didn't deserve help – I knew that – but what about that voice? Was that a new revelation? *Is it true? Everyone who calls on the name of the Lord will be saved... Could that be true for me?*

Unable to shake these thoughts or even come up with any new ideas, I knew that I just had to withdraw, to find solitude. For days on end – nearly two weeks – I isolated myself from everyone and just dwelt in my bedroom. Day and night I could find no peace. I just could not shake off the overwhelming acknowledgment of being guilty, convicted of all my selfish, evil acts. My thoughts would shift from knowing I was hell-bound to feeling psychotic. Was I just a crazy, messed-up 'acid'-head?

"If you are there, God, help me! If you can, God, help me! If you even *want* to help me, if there's any hope in you, God, please give me a sign! Anything that shines light and direction in this hellish life of mine. I need a sign, God!" I cried out again and again. "I don't even know who you are, let alone that you could, or even want to, really answer me. I don't know what to do, where to go, how to even find out who you are. I'm lost, *so lost.* I need to know, I need a sign to show who you are. I need a sign. I NEED A SIGN! *Please* give me a sign!"

"Glenn, Cockle's here for you!" my mum called up to me, breaking into my solitude one Monday night.

Cockle was a good old friend. We'd grown up together on the same estate, drunk, smoked dope and dropped trips together many times. We also shared a drug round, a door-to-door motorbike-powered delivery service on the south borders of London and District.

"Where you been? Ain't seen you around for weeks," Cockle enquired.

"Nothing much; just getting a bit of head space," I answered

"Yeah, I get like that. Come on, we're going around Barney's; he's got a few ounces of Red Seal that we need to try out," Cockle informed me.

"Nice!" was my reply. I needed to get stoned, have a laugh, change the terrible, repetitive tune in my mind...

Cockle put a joint together and we walked off to Barney's flat.

Barney and his girlfriend were pleased to see us. Lyne went off to put the kettle on as Barney with a huge grin pulled up a brown paper bag from behind his chair. "Got something special for you, Glenn," he smiled. "Help yourself! Got loads of 'acid'." He took an 'acid' tab out and ate it straight away.

Lyne promptly came from the kitchen, grabbed the bag, took out a blotter and swallowed it, then passed the bag to Cockle.

Cockle, smiling, said, "Nice one!" then did the same and passed the bag to me.

"Er, no thanks," I answered.

The three of them went silent, clearly shocked.

"What – you sick or something?" Barney enquired. It was very unusual and really out of character for me to refuse drink or drugs, especially 'acid', whatever time of day or night. "You'd better skin up then!" he laughed, throwing me a huge slab of 'black'[3].

"Red Seal... lovely stuff!" I smiled back.

I loved the smell of resin, as much as the whole ritual of putting a joint together. I set about making a huge speciality joint, for an evening devoted to getting as stoned as possible. The making of this joint gave me relief for a few minutes from the soul-churning anxiety.

Lyne switched the TV channel to watch a documentary on modern-day witchcraft.

"You're into this, aren't you?" Barney asked.

"*Was,*" I clarified.

"Leave it on. I'm interested in this; it's only white magic," said Lyne.

"Same thing as black magic. It's all got its roots in satanism; it's all dangerous," I insisted.

"Hang on, Cockle. This can't be the real Glenn Walsh. We've got a body snatcher here! No to free 'acid'? Seeing danger?" laughed Barney.

"Skin up, then," I said throwing the slab of resin to Perry, pushing my intention to get as stoned as possible.

---

[3] cannabis resin

The documentary was all about sanitising witchcraft as a harmless alternative religion, while showing lots of naked girls.

"Looks like fun to me! Cor!" laughed Barney.

I was getting very stoned while the others started tripping. In my mind the battle continued, a dialogue of thoughts, guilt, panic, a deep sense of being lost... "God, is there any way to you?" I was asking.

Suddenly I was drawn to look at the wood grain pattern on Barney's living room door. I could clearly see a bearded face: nose, mouth and eyes that looked piercingly sad. On the head I could see a crown which looked like it was made of thorns, and above that was the shape of a cross. The 'new voice' spoke again: "Knock and the door will be opened to you; for all who seek find and to anyone who knocks, the door will be opened."[4] The words echoed in my mind. I was startled.

"Look at the door – there's a face! A detailed face! It's the face... the face *of Jesus*. It's the face of Jesus!" I shouted excitedly.

"Where? What!" they all resounded.

"There – *here*, on your door!" I answered them, pointing it out, showing the eyes and the details patterned out in the wood grain.

"Oh, I can see it! That's blooming spooky!" said Lyne.

"It's the trip," Perry tried to reassure us. "We're all hallucinating; it won't be there later." He forced a laugh.

"I'm not tripping. Look, it's here in the pattern of the grain; it goes all the way through on the other side of the door," I insisted, examining the door on both sides.

"That's just weird. No one has ever noticed that before," Barney stated.

Everyone got up and looked closely at the door. "This is gonna be one weird trip!" laughed Perry.

Lynne passed me another joint.

"Nice one!" I said taking it, but I felt hope once again pour into my mind. I had asked God for a sign and there it was, right in front of my eyes: the face of Jesus. "I'm knocking, God; open the door to me," I repeated in my head as I slowly drifted off to a heavy cannabis-induced sleep.

I awoke in the morning to a panic, slumped in an armchair. I quickly looked towards the door. It was still there, the pattern of wood grain was in the shape of Jesus. *It is really there!*

---

[4] See Matthew 7:7-8.

"Look, the face of Jesus! It's still there!" I said excitedly.

"That's too spooky!" answered Lyne gruffly.

I had asked God to show me the way to him, the way to find peace, and there it was, a sign telling me to seek out Jesus. A new journey was about to start for me, a new direction to go in. But I had no idea where to go or where to start from, how or whom to ask.

I walked home that morning smiling; once again hope had come to me, invading the darkness. *Knock and the door shall be opened, seek and you will find! For everyone who seeks finds, and to all who knock, the door will be opened!*

My life was about to take on new meaning, with a new road to walk on – but to explain how I had got here in the first place, we need to cover some further background in the following chapters.

CHAPTER THREE

A Good Start

I was happy. I mean, *really* happy. We had just moved into our brand new bungalow which was in walking distance of our favourite beach. I even had my own bedroom for the first time.

I was just seven years old and the most popular boy in the school – it was official! One lunchtime during play, the whole school had gathered together to catch the most popular boy and girl and make them kiss. I was on the run, and although I was actually looking forward to getting caught, I put up a good pretence. My best friend was Jamie; although he was in a different class to me, we would meet up every breaktime and play 'motorcycles', running up and down the school field and speeding up to a sprint as we flew down the hills. I felt so free. I was attending school at St Mewans in Sticker and I was very slight, short and skinny; this was already the third school that I had attended when I started there at the age of six. Brendan, my older brother, encouraged me on my first day as he could see I was very anxious, but within minutes of walking into the schoolyard I was given the ultimate type of protection a young boy could get. Phil Carter, the school tough nut, had called a meeting in the middle of the playground, gathering every child to listen; he then, for a reason unbeknown to me, pointed directly at me and shouted out, "This kid is under my protection. If anyone messes with him, he messes with me! You got that?" Brendan looked at me and said, "What makes you so popular?" To be honest I didn't have a clue, but life was good.

I suppose I was a bit of a strange child. I refused to go to any form of nursery school when old enough, and then for the first few weeks of primary school in Kent I held my ground by standing alone in the corridor rather than participating in lessons. I'm not sure if I was rebellious, extremely insecure or just a bit special, but already at the age of five I had circled the globe and faced two near-death experiences.

The first incident that shook me was in Wollongong, Australia.

We had emigrated due to a few family tensions and started a new life in a hostel community while waiting to gain our Australian citizenship. I have a few memories of my time there, such as times spent on the beach catching creatures out of rock pools. I remember feeling a bit freaked out by kites flying so high and then walking around Sydney, but to me the greatest sight in Sydney was the people on stilts; to me they looked so tall that they nearly touched the sky. Other memories include the smell of barbecues, very different from how they smell in the UK; a very heavy rain storm in which the rain actually hurt; the sound of a kookaburra; oh yes, and of course *flies*, millions of them everywhere. Brendan and I often got into trouble for playing over the creek – not surprisingly, as the place was full of crocodiles, quicksand and the occasional shark, but you tell a young lad that and then try to stop him exploring... well, good luck with that! Two games we loved to play were marbles and 'splitzes'. My dad soon put an end to 'splitzes' because it included us throwing knives, and being a poor shot, I threw a large knife into Bren's leg instead of near it to make him do the splits.

Our time in Australia came to an abrupt end due to a near fatal car crash. Fortunately we were in an old Volkswagen Beetle that was built like a tank. Everyone else in the vehicle had cuts or broken bones. Brendan had been thrown through the windscreen but had only broken his collar bone. The emergency services couldn't believe that we had all survived, but I came out totally unscathed, not even a scratch. The shock, though, was too much for my mother to get over and she needed to return to England. So we left by ship one year earlier than my father, as he had to stay on in Australia and raise the finances to resettle us back in the UK. Six weeks at sea... I loved it! The strange sights of flying fish, dolphins and whales, just looking at miles and miles of sea with no land... The impact of this journey left me for most of my childhood with a huge desire to escape to a naval life.

Then, after arriving back in England, I was playing in my nan's garden alone. I had just been given a boiled sweet by my nan and told to suck it slowly so as not to choke on it. I remember running around, then taking a deep breath and feeling the sweet swoop down into my throat and lodge in my windpipe. *I'll just cough it up again,* I thought, but it was stuck. I tried again to cough it up but it would not budge. Panic hit. I was alone in the garden; I couldn't get a breath, try as hard as I could; I couldn't call out for help. I could feel my head start to spin so I bolted toward the back of the house up the steps, then pushing open the back door I flew into the kitchen. My mother, nan and Aunt Lilly were sitting around the table chatting so I tried to get their attention, but I couldn't say a word. I felt trapped, unable to breathe, unable to communicate, not knowing what to do, so I just stood there wide-eyed. The three of them turned and just looked at me, asking what I wanted – until I turned blue and passed out.

Aunt Lilly was a strong, dominant woman and used to taking control, so while my mum and nan went into meltdown, she got up, picked me up by one of my feet using just one of her hands, then, hanging me upside-down, she bashed me violently on the back with her other hand until the boiled sweet dislodged and fell out of my throat onto the floor. After a couple more 'whacks', I took in a large breath and began a quick recovery. She literally saved my life and took great pleasure in reminding me every time we met from then on.

These events haunted me, and I felt a driven desire to flaunt with death mixed with sporadic times of sheer panic that would engulf me, consuming my every thought.

Once my dad returned from Australia, our reunited family moved to Cornwall, and Cornwall became my playground. Brendan and I felt that we had no boundaries and would go out exploring for miles. Once we got so lost that I had to knock on a stranger's door and ask the man who answered how to get back to where we lived. He looked shocked to see us young boys, Brendan being the eldest aged eight, lost over ten miles from home. He kindly offered to drive us home, so we piled into his car and got a lift. It was all so innocent and he was just a kind stranger, but my dad was furious as we explained what we had been up to. We were told to stay closer to home, and to be honest there was enough to keep us amused close to our doorstep.

The beach provided miles of cliffs to climb. Even just walking along the edge of the clifftops looking down was great fun, especially the time I found a large, dead bird of prey which I was sure was an eagle, although it could have been a falcon of some sort. As soon as we saw it lying near the edge of the cliffs, I had an inspirational thought. There were three of us – Brendan, his friend Paul and me. They wanted to play football using the dead bird as the ball, but my plan was far superior, I believed. I grabbed the bird (it was still fresh and limp, so it could only have been dead a few hours at the most) and I ran off with it, with Paul and Bren in hot pursuit. They tried to get it off me, so I told them my plan and they liked it. We walked on together, laughing and peering over the cliff looking for our prey... Eventually I found the suitable victims, where an opening in the cliffs made for a sheer drop some fifty feet or more straight down. It was a nice, hot summer's day and a family group had settled on the beach below for a picnic. I was about to provide the entertainment and a topic for conversation that I was sure they would remember forever. Positioning myself so as to have a clear shot, I threw the eagle out into the air. It plummeted straight down, landing with a thud in the middle of all the group, right on the food and picnic blanket. We quickly retreated to avoid being seen, but remained in earshot of all the screaming and shouts of excitement coming from below. We howled with laughter for hours, going over the events and inventing different scenarios as to how we thought our victims must have experienced the prank.

It was around this time that I had my first encounter on the wrong side of the law. To us it was just innocent play, and the fact that the tracks that we chose to play on formed the main train route to Cornwall just added to the excitement. The train track ran along the clifftops that had become our play area; they were easily accessible and offered a scope of activities. We could sit near the tracks and watch the trains zoom past us, or put things on the tracks like old toys or stones and watch them zip into the air as the train wheels smashed into them, but my favourite activity was walking the live rails. I had been told that these rails carried enough electricity to kill you. If you put just one foot on them with your other foot on the ground, you would die instantly. Instead, you had to jump on the rail with both feet at the same time, keep your balance, and walk the line without putting a foot wrong, then exit both feet jumping clear of the rail, all the while realising that if one foot would slip off onto the ground you would be dead. I held the record for walking this live rail. I loved the challenge of flaunting with death, fighting off the temptation to put one foot down just to see what would happen and the feeling of adrenaline pumping through my system, all the time keeping alert to a chinking sound in the line that meant a train was approaching at high speed. When we heard this sound we would have to jump and run to the edge of the track. On one such occasion as we ran to the side of the track, a police officer suddenly appeared and grabbed me. After he gave us a few words about how dangerous and stupid we were, he then took us home in his car. After a long chat with our parents, he drove away and we had to face a very angry dad ready to drive home to us a message of

"Never play on those rails again!" Wow – my dad knew how to make sure we never did that again!

We soon replaced the train track with tree-climbing, and visits to the local building sites that offered adventure after adventure, but our happiness and home life was beginning to crumble.

CHAPTER FOUR

I Hate This God!

Every night now the arguing would start. At first I'd hear them shouting after I'd gone to bed – my parents would wake me up with their shouting at each other. Then it increased to every mealtime or, even sooner, immediately as my dad came home from work.

One time a mug just missed my dad's head and shattered on the wall, spraying his shoulder with hot tea and broken splinters of china; then, after throwing this, my mum hurled accusation after accusation at him. She then turned to me and Brendan and shouted, "He's having an affair! He's seeing another woman!"

"No, Mum, no!" we both cried back before being sent to our rooms. She was really coming apart, but we couldn't believe her. *Not my dad; he wouldn't do that. Not him.*

I never felt close to my dad. After all, I was the mistake, not planned for like Brendan. This was always very clear and noticeable to everyone, but I got over most of the feelings of rejection – my mum made sure of that. But now she was falling apart... My dad had been the religious rock of our family. He made sure that we were exposed to Roman Catholicism and insisted we went to church schools, whether they were Catholic or Church of England. In addition, he would conclude every day by calling out to me and Bren as we went to bed each night, "Goodnight! God bless! Don't forget to say your prayers..."

I did believe that God was real and that he was there to answer our prayers and help us when we were in crisis. I understood the Scriptures during religious education at school, and was moved deeply and emotionally while singing in the school choir at Truro Cathedral. Instinctively each night, while alone listening to my parents shouting at each other, I would cry out to this God of my father, "Stop my parents hating each other! Make them love each other again! Don't let them separate! Please, God, keep us all together as a family." But my mum seemed to be going insane, and my dad retreated and distanced himself even more from us.

I could never claim to being a good kid, but my behaviour at school during this time went from bad to worse in a dramatically short time. I was now fighting my friends; I shut down in the lessons and wouldn't talk; and instead of playing with Jamie, I took to stealing confiscated toys from the teachers' drawers at breaktimes, as well as continually plotting ways to cause damage or disruption. Eventually, I got caught for various things and was kept under the close scrutiny of one particular teacher, Mr Hicks. He kept me on curfew, and I was on constant report and restraint, only being allowed out in certain parts of the playground that could be seen by the staff room under his continual watchful eyes.

Outside of school I was freer to cause trouble, and on a Saturday morning I'd typically be dropped at the local cinema club. During one particular week I'd collected up a stack of small tubes of oil paints – over thirty of them. Somehow I managed to sneak into the cinema before anyone else and, under the cover of darkness, I placed the open paint tubes randomly on any chair I could make stay down. (The old cinema seats could flip up and down.) Then the droves of children came steaming through the doors, running for the best seats and quickly sitting on them. Spurts of paint were going off all over the auditorium, while I sat in my seat laughing. Only Brendan, who was sitting next to me, knew what was going on and giggled away with me. Of course, the news of the chaos I had caused was reported back to all the local schools including mine, and I was the main suspect. Mr Hicks called me into his office and accused me of being the paint-spreader; he even told me that one of my friends had reported on me. I admitted nothing – no one knew except Bren, and I knew he wouldn't 'grass me up' on this – but I was no longer the popular boy in anyone's eyes.

My parents had now argued regularly for over a year. I was eight years old and my happiness was gone. This God whom I cried out to each night just remained silent. If he was real, he evidently wasn't interested in my world. I really thought God answered prayers; wasn't that what this Christian stuff was all about?

I examined the state of my family: we had the new bungalow near the beach, my dad had gone through promotions and was now head of a department, and my mum was also working at a nearby factory, so money wasn't that scarce; *but there was no joy.* The daily accusations of my dad's continuing affair, my mum consoling herself through drink... none of us could take it any more. My mum was extremely attractive and a caring woman; why would my dad be unfaithful to her? *Surely she is just imagining it all,* everyone thought – but she had found earrings in her bed that weren't hers, and her friends were reporting back that they'd seen him with a "cat's eyes woman", as my mum referred to her.

Enough was enough! We were leaving. My mum could no longer stay with my dad and was taking me and Bren to live with her parents back in Dartford, Kent. I was now aged nine, and my father had offered to drive us to Kent. We all sat in the car for the long, silent journey; it was during a harsh winter but even the snow falling for the whole trip could not provoke excitement in any of our bones.

After we arrived, my dad gave a short farewell and then drove off. That was that; my mum's marriage over, the Walsh family split. Bren and I were to live at my grandparents' small, two-bedroomed council house, with mum just down the road living with my 'Great Granma'.

I went up alone to my new shared bedroom. Looking upwards I said, "Well, God, if you *are* real, you're crap. If you don't care about me, well, I don't care about you. Shove your religion!" In fact, that is a very tame version of what I actually said, as I had learned quite a few swear words by that age and I emptied a whole rally of them towards this God of my father. I now actually hoped he wasn't real and that all this religious stuff was just nonsense, as the alternative seemed to be that this God didn't 'give a stuff' about me. It didn't take long for hatred and resentment to take a deep root in my heart. I'd seen my mother torn to shreds and my whole world destroyed.

Then, after a few weeks of living at my grandparents', I found an old Bible, which surprised me as they weren't at all religious. I took this book upstairs; then, making sure I was alone, I spouted another torrent of abuse towards God and tore the book in two, throwing it across the room. "So, 'crappy God', I'll do my life alone then," I called out to this apparently non-existent entity. With this new directive decision so early on in my life, I began my journey of self-destruction.

CHAPTER FIVE

Sean

The transition back to Our Lady's Roman Catholic School in Kent was okay, although Bren seemed to struggle more than me, which was unusual. We soon settled in at my grandparents' but it was hard with my mum not living with us.

Mum was getting friendly with a man called Sean. He'd been around for a while at family scenes, as he was a close friend to a cousin of someone, so he wasn't a complete stranger to my mum. I didn't like their budding friendship though, as I was still hoping that she'd go back to my dad. I still considered Dad a victim – but another shock lay ahead.

The summer holidays were approaching, and Brendan and I were to spend a week in our old home with Dad in Cornwall. We travelled by coach from Victoria, London to be met by him in Exeter in his new Ford Capri. *Wow!* I was duly impressed; it was a purple sports car with a black vinyl covered roof. But after sitting for hours on that boring coach, it was hard to get too excited by another two-hour car journey.

When we arrived, it felt so weird walking around the bungalow. It was so empty and lifeless. My old bedroom furniture was gone and in the middle of the room a camp bed had been set up, but on my wall still hung a picture of a spacecraft circling the moon, something familiar – an old memory created warmth in my heart.

The start of our holiday was fantastic. Every day we'd go off to the beach, climb cliffs and dive off them into the sea. We ate in a Chinese restaurant and we'd go off to the social club every evening, and generally had a great time. Then, near the end of the week, my dad informed us that we were going to meet his friend Sam at the club that evening. Sam worked with him and was a good friend, he told us.

I wondered what Sam would turn out to be like, as my dad had made such a big deal about meeting him during our journey to the club. Then Sam arrived and walked over to our table – but Sam wasn't at all what I'd imagined. *Sam was short for Samantha!*

It was the woman my mum had described so many times. I recognised her by her 'cat's eyes'! She resembled the singer Eartha Kit, with bright green eye shadow plastered over her eyelids.

I didn't know how to react. Truth be told, I was in a state of shock and felt so weak, but I couldn't upset my dad so I tried to act politely for the whole evening. For the last couple of days she joined us – on the beach, on a boat trip and at the club. Although I pretended to enjoy these times together, inside I was filling with hatred towards them both: my dad, the lying, adulterous hypocrite; and her, the cat woman.

I had returned home to mum but I felt confused. On the one hand my dad looked so alone, the bungalow so empty. On the other hand there was this 'Sam Cat's Eyes' – my mum had been right all along.

I began to sob, sitting alone in the garden, until my mum walked out and saw me.

"Why are you crying?" she asked, concerned.

I tried as best I could to explain, but it all came out wrong – as though I were feeling sorry for my dad.

"Are you taking sides with that monster?" she cried. "He's got everything: the bungalow, *everything!* He doesn't care about us! Did you know he had a party after we left because she now lives with him? Oh, he's put on a good act, but he's happy with his new life of freedom!"

She then told me how her old neighbours had kept in touch with her, informing her of everything that had been going on at her old home. I recoiled as my mind flashed through the events of our holiday. He *had* removed us from his life, she was right; all the photos of Bren and me were gone from every room, our furniture and toys were gone... Where *was* it all? I took hold of my emotions and stemmed the tears. Love? I didn't want any more of love, this stupid emotion that just causes hurt... *Get out of my heart; I'm not crying any more,* I said to myself. I made an inner vow to harden my heart from this time onward.

I soon found out where all my old toys had ended up: my cars, my Scalextric, my golfer, my bike... He'd given the lot to his girlfriend's niece and nephew. This revelation helped me to re-form my tender broken heart to a hardened shell that couldn't be damaged so easily again.

I then decided to support my mum's friendship with Sean – hey, he was nice to us and would take us out most weekends to exciting places including London Zoo and Chessington theme park; he seemed to understand family in a way my own dad never had. Then we went together for a family holiday to a holiday centre near Portsmouth, during which my mum informed us that we were all going to move in with Sean at his house in Penge near Crystal Palace. It felt like we were becoming a family again: Mum, Bren and me all living in the same house.

We soon settled into a new way of 'doing family'. It all seemed to be going well, we made friends, and Crystal Palace Park was less than a ten-minute walk away. That said, I didn't really fit into my new school. Once again it was a Catholic Church school, St Joseph's, so I had to keep secret the fact that my mum was separated from her husband and now living with another man; plus, from my first day I was ridiculed by the other kids for my still-strong Cornish accent. I only made one friend from my class, who had been bullied by the others, but after school I would usually hang about with Brendan and his friends.

With this older group London now became our haunt, visiting museums, riding on trains, ice-skating and making camps in the huge dinosaurs scattered around the grounds of Crystal Palace Park. These dinosaur statues were over twenty feet high, hollow with open hatches underneath their bellies which gave us access, although to get to them we had to negotiate our way over ponds and fences as they were off bounds to the public. Our trips out were in no way educational; we just wanted to find places to cause disruption and chaos, and we often found ourselves being chased by gangs of older youths when we ventured through their estates.

I seemed to have tasked myself in becoming an irritant to everyone and everything around me, even at home. Sean's house was actually a maisonette. From the outside it looked like one house but in reality the building was split into two self-contained dwellings, one being on the ground floor and with us living upstairs. The fact that living underneath me were another couple opened a door for me to cause them problems. It was nothing personal; sadly, they just flashed on my 'give them grief' radar. Whenever we found ourselves alone, Bren and I decided that rather than walk around from room to room, it was better to jump; that way we could cause a consistent banging and thudding which would drive our downstairs neighbours to bang back on their ceiling. Once we got our desired knocking, we would increase our jumping. The best annoyance though was when the man of the house sat in his garden trying to read his paper. We would position ourselves above him, making sure we had a good aim to drop frozen peas into his open paper, and then we would watch them roll down to his lap. Time and again we would do this and he never flinched, moaned or even moved to another location, so I upped our game and used pickled onions instead. Sadly, he just moved his paper-reading to indoors.

But there was a hidden side to our new family, that was about to explode and cause yet again another dramatic change. It all came out when my nan paid us a visit on a Saturday morning. While Sean was out shopping, my mum confided to her that he was secretly violent towards her. She showed my nan the bruises that covered her body. Bren and I were just kicking a ball around in the garden, oblivious to what was going on, when suddenly we heard a scream and a kafuffle coming from indoors. We both ran in. Sean had returned home and was standing near the door with blood flowing down his face from what looked like scratch marks running across his right cheek. My nan, like her sister Lilly, was a strong woman who would not put up with this kind of nonsense, so Sean's actions had caused him to encounter her wrath.

After a while we were all sat together and it looked as though we would be moving back to live with our grandparents – but Sean became very apologetic and through tears promised to change. He even suggested that we could *all* move back to my grandparents' hometown. He offered to sell up and buy a new home for us.

Sean was true to his word and put the maisonette on the market that very day. The next few months were mixed with excitement and anxiety. We had moved to live with Sean at the start of my final year at primary school, and now I was due to start secondary school after the holidays. I knew that once we moved house, I would have to transition to yet another school.

I began secondary school in Bromley and immediately had a friendship base with Brendan's friends whom I had already hung about with. I also made a few friends from my class as we travelled by train together to and from school. On the trains we would cause as much damage and chaos as we possibly could. I'd unscrew the lightbulbs and throw them out of the windows, aiming at people standing on the platforms of the stations that we didn't stop at, then as firework night approached we'd get on the train armed with bangers and rockets. We'd let the fireworks off in the carriages and hide in the baggage rails as they whizzed and exploded all around us. Then I took it further by throwing bangers onto the platforms, causing people to scatter.

This came to a dramatic conclusion when one time, as we were parked next to another train, I noticed the train had a fairly large open window, so I opened ours and called out to a man standing in the other train, "'scuse me, mister. Hey, mister!"

"Yes?" he answered.

"Here you are!" I said, leaning out of my window and passing him something in my right hand.

At first he went to take what I had in my hand. It was a lighted banger, which I then threw through the open windows into his carriage. Our train pulled away and we all fell about laughing. Unknown to us, though, he had recognised our school uniform, and he subsequently informed our school about the incident. It didn't take long for our headmaster to work out who the culprits were, as we were the only group that travelled on that train to our school.

The headmaster called the seven of us to line up outside his office; one by one the others were marched into his room while we stood outside hearing the whooshing sound of the cane and cries of our friends being struck by it. As we waited our turn, I turned to Brendan and said, "Sod this, I'm off. Only an idiot would queue to get whacked." I simply walked out of the school, Brendan followed and we went home. The timing for us seemed perfect as Sean and my mum received mixed news that day; not only did the school inform them of the incident and our walking out, but we also got our moving date which was just the following week. My mum tried to force me and Bren to go back to school and face our punishment. Brendan went, but I was too slippery and managed to avoid going in. Then we moved to our new house and things looked pretty good – for a short time anyway.

CHAPTER SIX

The Shadow of Darkness

The new house seemed very nice indeed: a three-bed, large, semidetached 1930s build. It was on what we considered the 'posh side' of town, about half an hour's walk from the council estate where my grandparents lived. Brendan, being the smart one, was accepted at a local grammar school, but I failed the entry exam so once again had to endure Catholic school education.

My school was over an hour's bus journey away, a long, boring trip on a number 480 double-decker green bus. Once again I had to make new friends, and for the first two days of school I tried to fit in. Then on day three I was a bit lost and confused as to where the classroom was that I was expected to be in.

I asked another pupil, who informed me that my classroom was upstairs, so being a little late I ran up the first flight of stairs that I passed. As I did so, I was brought to a sudden stop by a booming irate shout of, "Hey, you boy, where do you think you're going? Stop right where you are!"

I stopped and turned around to face whomever this was and said, "I'm going to class, sir."

"No, you're not," he bellowed at me angrily. "Come down here and follow me!"

I walked down to where he was and followed him, not knowing what was going on.

"What makes you think you can just run up the staff stairs?" he questioned me as we quickly strode along the corridors to his office.

"I'm sorry, sir, but I'm new here. I didn't know they were staff stairs," I answered.

"I'll give you a lesson in remembering," he gruffed as we entered his office. He opened a cupboard and took out a long, dark cane, then directed me, "Put your hand out flat."

I did as he asked, then *swoosh* – three whacks of the cane across my hand, striking my palm, my thumb and my fingers.

I tried to hold back the tears as searing pain went through my right hand.

"So, boy, what do you say?"

"I didn't know," I answered.

He looked at me blankly and said, "The correct answer is, 'Sorry, sir, it won't happen again.'" Then he just stood there waiting for my correct reply.

"Sorry, sir," I mumbled.

"Better get to class then," he concluded dismissing me.

I walked off and found the boys' toilets, just wanting to run my throbbing hand under the cold tap to ease the stinging and also to wipe away my stupid tears. As I ran my hand under the tap, another lad walked in and laughed. "Just been caned by old Harry Hawket! He's an old git! Mind you, not as bad as Mr Reece; he whacks you at the top of the leg just under your bum. Now, that *does* bloody hurt. What did you do then?" he asked.

"I just walked up the staff stairs, and being new here I didn't even know they were just for staff," I answered.

"What? The stupid git! They ain't bloody staff stairs. I think he's just taken a dislike to you. Anyway, it's nearly breaktime – so just hang about in here then go for lunch. See yer around." He then left me alone.

What the hell was that all about then? I wondered. The only conclusion that dawned on me was that my old headmaster must have informed on me and I had now got what was coming to me, although I never did find out for sure.

I put this incident behind me, and for the first few months at St John's Comprehensive School I tried to be an 'okay pupil'.

Our new house was nice at first. I had my own bedroom, Mum and Sean were getting on, and Bren and I had only fallen out with one neighbour because he had tried to chase us out of the alleyway leading to our garage next to our house. We were getting our own back on him for throwing a brick in our direction and shouting at us to "clear off", by making him a target for many a prank.

But something wasn't quite right in this new home. Unusual and unnerving occurrences began to disturb our peace. At first we all thought it was our imaginations running riot, but even our dog Tiny, a Jack Russell Terrier, joined in our paranoia. Tiny would often sit at the bottom of stairs which led to our bedrooms and would just stare up the stairs growling and barking at nothing. Sometimes she would yelp as if she had just been hurt and come running into the front room. Often a weird anxiety-filled, heavy atmosphere would engulf us; we would all feel it at the same time even when we were in different rooms. It became common to find either me or Brendan asleep on the floor of each other's bedrooms after a disturbed night.

My mum hated being alone in the house, as she would experience things moving around; even though she has been extremely deaf since the age of three, she was certain that she could hear the sound of stomping up and down the stairs. Then she found a pair of her shoes placed at the bottom of the stairs even though she was sure that she had put them in her bedroom wardrobe. I often thought that I saw a shadowy figure flit past the top of the stairs as I walked past on the bottom, so I took to sticking my fingers up and insulting what I called "the shadow man" as I walked past through the hallway.

Then one Saturday morning I came out of the front room and saw what I thought was Brendan run past the top of the stairs.

"Glenn!" I thought he called out, as I heard his bedroom door slam.

"What you up to?" I called back, thinking that he had just run out of my mum's bedroom.

I then ran up to look for him.

Pushing his bedroom door open, I entered and called out, "Where are you hiding, you idiot?" as I couldn't see him anywhere.

I searched under his bed and looked in his wardrobe, then I suddenly heard my bedroom door open and shut.

I ran out of Bren's room, down the corridor and flew into mine saying, "You idiot!" but he wasn't in there either.

My room was at the very back of the house, so I looked out of my window into the back garden. To my panic, I saw Bren, Sean and my mum all sitting in the garden playing with Tiny. I turned to flee my room, but as I tried to open the door it felt as though it was being pulled the other way. I tugged and tugged until eventually it opened, and I just ran into the garden.

"Were you upstairs just then?" I asked Brendan.

"When? Why? What's up?" he asked.

"Nothing... just thought I heard you up there," I said but then realised there was no way he could have got into the garden without passing me; plus, he was already there when I looked out of my window.

A short while after this I had a terrifying nightmare. I dreamt that I was standing at the foot of the stairs poking my fingers up and taunting, as I was in the habit of doing, when suddenly at the top of the stairs appeared the shadow man. He was tall, covered in darkness, and he just stood there. Although I couldn't see his face, I could feel him staring down at me. The dream seemed so real. I could feel that strange atmosphere, fear gripped me, and then he swooped down towards me. Suddenly I awoke with a jump, then jumped again as Brendan burst into my room.

"Can I sleep on your floor, bruv? Did you hear that banging? The dog's wet itself downstairs; sounded like someone's been running up and down the stairs," he blurted out, clearly spooked.

"Yes, sure," I answered, jumping again as I didn't realise Tiny was in Bren's hands and she jumped onto my bed to settle by my feet.

Later that week, after eating my tea alone as I was a bit late home from school, I walked into the front room to join the others. The front room was just left at the foot of the stairway and had a glass single-panelled door. This door was already opened so I just walked in, stood for a second to see where I could sit to watch TV, then suddenly I heard a loud thud. Startled, I turned to see what it was, when the door slammed shut with such force that the panel shattered, showering me with fragments of broken glass. Fortunately I wasn't hurt, but Sean's reaction was quite alarming.

With anger in his eyes towards me, he blurted out, "Why on earth do you have to slam doors? Guess I'll have to clear up all the damage!" He pushed me out of the way as he stormed out of the room.

Mum, Bren and I just looked at each other, with no clue as to what had just happened.

Sean would not entertain any of our conversations about anything we considered supernatural. But he was becoming noticeably very moody; he would often just snap for apparently no reason. The strange thing was that just before he exploded with a temper tantrum, the whole atmosphere of the room would change; we could physically feel that something was about to happen. A kind of coldness would sweep in. And when I say he'd have a tantrum, it wasn't that he'd start shouting; it was more calm and demonstrative than just that.

One time we were all sitting in the front room when such an incident occurred. Spontaneously we all turned to look at him, he mumbled something, then he tightened his grip on the glass pint jug he had in his right hand. This jug was made of thick, clear glass, covered in one-inch dimpled, squared patterns, typical of pint jug glasses used in many pubs. Suddenly the jug exploded under the sheer force of his grip, and liquid and glass flew all around his hand. Remarkably, he was totally uninjured; he walked off laughing and mumbling out of the room and just went upstairs to bed. We sat there stunned, and I must admit I have tried many times unsuccessfully to shatter a glass like he did that night; I am convinced it is humanly impossible.

We never knew what would trigger these episodes, but another time we all felt the strange atmospheric change and Sean calmly got up out of his chair, picked up a wooden broom, snapped it in two, then placed the two parts of the broken handle together and snapped them again into four pieces. Finally, he just threw them out of the room and calmly walked off to his bedroom once again.

He had started being physically cruel to my mum again, but she kept it a closer secret this time, until one night I woke up and heard a scream coming from downstairs. I ran down into the front room to find Sean holding the limp body of my mum with one hand grasped around her neck. When he saw me – this wimpy, small, not-yet-twelve-year-old kid – he grinned and just dropped her still body at my feet, then pushed past me walking off once again up to his bedroom. For a few seconds I thought she was dead, but fortunately she soon stirred. I was determined to call the police but somehow she managed to dissuade me.

From that time on, Sean's violent attentions were focussed towards me as well as my mum, and life got that bit harder.

Then one regular morning, while as usual we were getting ready for school, my mum whispered to Bren and me, "Get ready for school but don't go anywhere."

"What's going on?" we whispered back.

"Shh," she said. Sean was hovering around getting ready to leave for work, then as soon as he left, my mum ran to the window and watched him drive away into the distance. "Quick! We are off!" she said directing us to load her car up with as much of our stuff as we could.

We then fled, turning up once again at my grandparents' house, right back where we had been before the Sean episode, just a little more bruised, disillusioned and angry for the paths that our lives were going down.

It didn't take Sean long to find out where we were. For a while he tried to convince us to move back, but fortunately he'd had his second chance and my mum was all the wiser. He soon got the message that reconciliation was not on my mum's agenda and his life moved on in a different direction – as did ours too when, after two years of living with my grandparents, the council offered us a home of our own.

CHAPTER SEVEN

Mad Dog

Our new house was literally around the corner. We lived on the same road of this large social housing estate. Although it seemed a small move, it was worlds apart; on this west side of the estate a large gang of youths hung about intimidating all the other kids, as well as the odd adult that upset them. Bren and I had been chased by them a few times when we had walked past the small park or alleyways in which they used to hang about. Even a few of the girls in that group looked mean and acted very aggressively. To survive on this part of the estate we had to work out how to become accepted and part of the gang.

We now lived directly opposite the ringleaders of this gang, Steve and Cockle. Steve had been in and out of Borstal most of his life as well as having a few short stints in prison now that he was over eighteen years of age. Cockle (a nickname) was the younger of these brothers and was nearly fifteen, Bren's age.

We got used to passing the gang and saying, "Alright?" At first they just mumbled back, but the more we saw them the more they seemed okay to us. Every afternoon I would have to walk past a crowd of them hanging about in the little park hidden through the alleyway on my journey home from school. At first I'd rush through, hoping I wouldn't get seen. A few times, however, Cockle called out, "Alright?" as I rushed passed, so I'd slow down my pace and call back, "Alright, mate?" Still, as yet we hadn't really spoken.

The breakthrough of introductions happened when the police came to visit my mum, telling her that I had been arrested. Instead of going to school, a school friend and I had broken into a sports pavilion and caused a lot of damage. The presence of the police caught Steve's attention, so one afternoon as I walked past the little park, he called out, "Hey,

Walshy brother, saw the police round yours the other day. What's happening?"

"Oh, they arrested me and charged me for burglary and arson," I called back.

"Come here," he directed me, so I walked over and joined the crowd gathered around him. "First offence?" he asked.

"Well, the first I've been arrested and charged for!" I laughed.

I spent the next few hours listening to Steve and the others sharing about all the things that they had been arrested for; most of them had been to Borstal or prison depending on their ages. They assured me that I wouldn't go down for a first offence, although they stressed with arson you can never tell. It seemed that I had finally been initiated into the group, and from that afternoon onwards I had become one of them.

I was in the gang and started to learn how to survive on the Tree estate. I was soon unlearning any remnant of decency that my parents had taught me and began to think like the 'pack', as I saw them. I was nearly fourteen and the world soon opened up into a life of drinking, smoking dope, music, stealing cars and, of course, girls.

The mid-1970s saw a revival of rock 'n' roll music, and because all our parents used to be rockers, we had all been exposed to the best that rock 'n' roll had to offer. Cockle, Bren, Eddie, Jim, Jimmy and I began to dress like Teddy Boys. Steve and the others all gave their approval and we really looked the part.

Unswerving in our new identities, we dressed like Teds regardless of where we went. It caused me a few problems at school. My new appearance clashed with the school uniform protocols, which meant on occasion I'd be sent home. I also stood out a bit too much and began to get hassled when I was alone at school from the new punks and skinheads – but I wouldn't conform for anyone. We began to get quite a reputation around our hometown and beyond, which we relished in even though it also brought us a lot of attention from the police.

On one of our stints around London we travelled back through Lewisham. As we walked through the streets, a group of rockabillies shouted over to us, then ran into the road and held back the traffic to let us pass by. "Nice one, boys!" they called out as we walked by. We put our thumbs up giving mutual approval. Then, on the bus journey home through Woolwich, a group of girls came 'upstairs' to where we were sitting. "Teddy Boys!" one of them called out as they walked up towards us. "Hey, do you know Glenn Walsh and Bren and Cockle and their gang?" they called to us.

"I am he," I answered feeling like the coolest fourteen-year-old teenager on the planet.

Again I had become Mr Popular, but soon picked up a nickname from the others that took months to shake off.

Typically, I was walking through the alley past the little park on my way home from school. In my hand was my orange Adidas sports bag that I used to carry things in.

"What's that? Are you a stiff? Carrying your schoolbooks to do some work for teacher, are you, Glenn?" Eddie called over to me. Everyone saw that I was getting irritated by the name 'stiff', so they all joined in calling me 'stiff'.

Truth was, I *did* have a schoolbag and I had a great need for it, but it wasn't for schoolwork. No, I was more enterprising than that. I had for a while been building up a client base at Bren's school for items requested. Brendan would bring from his school a list of things needed, and for a very competitive price I would provide them. I had worked out a way of getting my hands on anything they needed – from new textbooks to rulers, set squares, pens, pencils... whatever they dared put on the list. I carefully and regularly moved items from the school storeroom or staff rooms to my locker, from where I could load up my bag ready for Brendan to deliver at his end. Sadly though, someone 'grassed me up' after I'd become a bit too greedy. The teachers gathered around my locker. Then, when they managed to open it, there were looks of shock as they retrieved over three hundred retractable pencils. Once again, I was not only sent for the cane but also threatened with expulsion. Only after my mum's pleas of "Please, don't expel my son; you are the only ones doing him any good" did the school settle with me being kept on, but with the provision of being excluded from nearly half of the school's grounds.

With the loss of business, school now had no attraction to me at all. I very rarely went any more. Brendan got so good at forging letters that all the written correspondences from my school or the County Educational Department about my regular absences were filled and returned by him, so my mum never got to know. My grandad, though, had a good idea of what I was up to and suggested that every now and then I should go to work with him. He was a self-employed painter and decorator; I think he had a plan for me to one day take over his business as I took to the craft instantly, but I just saw it as an opportunity to earn a bit of cash, which at age fourteen came in very useful.

My nan later put a spanner in the works as she found out that Brendan and I were often drinking in one of the local pubs most afternoons instead of being at school. She barged into the 'Sally', as we called our local, shouted at the barman for serving us "underage children" and for a brief while put an end to this social engagement.

My teenage years seemed to last a lifetime and were filled with parties and fun times. Friday nights were spent at the Temple Hill under-eighteens disco. We had a routine built in place to make the evenings more fun. We'd arrive about an hour early and rip off the local off-licence, stealing crates of beer and any other alcohol we could slip out of the shop unnoticed. At the back of the centre, we knew, was a fire escape that we could stash the beers at, as we were usually searched on entry to the disco for weapons or drink. Then once we had gained entry, we could help ourselves to the free beer we had stashed within easy reach. Every event we were at was alcohol-fuelled; we found many ways to get drink into any occasion and they nearly always ended up with fights breaking out and us being at the centre of them.

On the odd occasion, when there seemed little to do, we would challenge the police to try to catch us. We'd phone them up from public phone boxes and tell them what we were up to. "Catch us if you can," we'd declare. We knew so many hideouts in the town and on the estates that no matter how many squad cars they sent out, again and again we would just slip away.

After too many taunts from us, the police took out a new weapon to catch us: police dogs, great big German Shepherds.

It was drawing close to midnight and about twenty of us had been walking around the town causing trouble. We then broke off into smaller groups with about half of the group deciding to go home. The rest of us were not yet ready and walked off towards the lakes to harass a few of the late night fishermen. Suddenly two police cars swooped around the corner at different ends of the street, hoping to box us in.

"Down the alley, quick!" Cockle shouted.

We loved the adrenaline caused from a police chase and soon the banter started.

"You'll never take me alive, copper!" I called out as we laughed and ran down the narrow, unlighted alleyway towards the lakes. We were pushing each other over and winding each other up as we ran.

I was running with Jimmy, Kev, Cockle and Bren; all of us were well paced together. We exited the alley onto a clearing and crossed a main road when another police vehicle came to an abrupt stop near to us. The back doors of the van flew open and out came two large German Shepherd dogs. Only one of them was on a leash; the other stood awaiting instructions, staring at us. We picked up the pace a bit more and strode across the road, ran through a tree-lined hedge and slipped down the steep bank into the grounds that held four large lakes.

As we negotiated our way down the bank, I was very aware of Jimmy being close behind me, when I heard him cry out. I looked back to see one of the dogs biting onto his arm and bringing him down to the ground. I had no idea where the other dog was, so as soon I found level ground I quickly climbed a tree, calling the others to follow me.

"The dog's got Jimmy," I told Cockle, Bren and Kev as they climbed up the tree to hide with me.

"Yeah, I saw it; it almost got me, so I pushed Jimmy into it," Kev answered.

We then went very quiet as a group of police officers gathered around the base of the tree. They were shining their torches over the waters and into the bushes all around us. I found the whole episode totally amusing and had to supress giggling.

"Watch this!" I whispered to the others

I then lowered myself by hanging on to a branch with both hands, so that my feet were hovering above the officers' heads. Everyone's eyes widened as I slowly did pull ups inches away from the oblivious group of police officers desperately searching for us. Then the officers just walked away into the pitch blackness and the others started to swear at me, during which time a new nickname emerged for me which this time stuck for years: Mad Dog.

CHAPTER EIGHT

Sweet Sixteen

My leaving school wasn't exactly an emotional episode. Exams were going on, and I decided to take them even though I was totally 'winging it'; I hadn't studied or even attended most of the lessons.

It was late May 1979, and my form tutor called me over.

"Sixteen this week, aren't you, Glenn?" Mr Blunt asked.

"Sure am!" I answered.

"Not worth you coming here any more then, is it?"

"S'pose not. I've finished my exams, so if it's all right with you, I'll be off today then," I declared,

"Okay, class, let's say goodbye to Glenn, shall we?" Mr Blunt called out.

A few of my classmates came over and we all said our goodbyes, but then, to my surprise, one of the 'swatty' girls came over, said, "What the hell..." and right there and then snogged me. Although I was totally unprepared, I enjoyed the moment. I collected up contact addresses from a few of the class, including hers, and then just left and headed home. As I got on the 480 bus for the last time, I just emptied my pockets of all the details that I had collected and decided to put the whole school episode behind me and move on to whatever was next.

By the age of sixteen I had had a string of girlfriends, but I now found myself completely unable to commit to any one relationship. Often at parties I'd go from one girl to another; I'd also upset a few of my friends by going with their girls. Once, while seeing one of my girlfriends, I was invited to a blind date to meet a girl who was very interested in me. I had to laugh when I met her for the first time, as it turned out to be my girlfriend's sister.

My main love, though, was drink. Almost every night I would go down the town to get extremely drunk with Eddie.

Amazingly, I walked straight into a decent job after leaving school and became an apprentice printer. The only reason I got the job was because I had phoned up on the same day that the person who had originally been offered the position declined it, so the disgruntled employer just gave it to me by default.

I started well in my new career and was very enthusiastic. I attended Print College in Holborn one day a week and enjoyed learning a host of new skills, using the Heidelberg letterpress machine as well as the lithographic printer and working in the darkroom.

Also, at college I'd noticed a character called Charlie, who was very popular and part of the punk scene. I'd heard from a few of the other students that he was a drug dealer, which put him on my 'must get to know' radar. So one morning at class, hoping to get Charlie's attention, I reached sneakily into my pocket and removed a small white pill-like mint from my pocket and held it in my fingers. I waited for Charlie to look my way; then, acting as suspiciously as could, I popped the mint quickly into my mouth, swallowing it instantly.

As I sat eating my lunch, Charlie came over and sat next to me. He was a very funny guy and had me laughing at some of his antics within seconds. He then leaned towards me and asked if I was "on anything".

"Need to be to get through the boredom of this place," I answered.

"What's your queen?" he then asked.

"'Speed'. Why, can you get me some? I've just popped my last one," I answered.

"Sure can. I can get you whatever you so desire." He laughed.

We were then joined by his mate Pete.

"Coming back to mine for a draw?" Charlie asked him.

"Yeah, sweet!" was Pete's immediate reply.

"Coming?" Charlie invitingly asked me as they both got up to leave.

Charlie lived on what he boasted to be the largest row of council flats in Europe, in the Old Kent Road, with his mother, who was fortunately at work, meaning we could sit in his flat and get very stoned.

We were having a laugh and smoking 'bush', which every now and then popped as the marijuana seeds exploded inside the joint, when for a brief while Charlie disappeared to another room. He returned smiling, holding a small, round black ball about three inches in diameter.

"Opium Golf Ball," he joyfully exclaimed through grinning teeth.

He cut the ball into two halves and with pure delight showed us the white centre of this black cannabis-resin-formed ball.

"Pure opium centred, with veins of opium running throughout," he boasted. "Ever had opium?" Charlie questioned me.

"Can't say I have," I answered in a gentlemanly manner.

"Well then, gents, shall I put one together, what, what?" Charlie laughed as he meticulously rolled one of the finest joints I had ever seen.

After that time with Charlie, I experienced one of the weirdest but most euphoric journeys alone as I headed home on the underground and train. Needless to say my supposed learning at The London College of Print went into decline from that afternoon onwards – as did my attendance at work. Sadly, the day-to-day commitment expected conflicted with my social life, and eventually one had to give way to the other.

The final straw came after I went to work looking like I had just about survived ten rounds stuck in the ring with a world champion heavyweight boxer. Two black eyes, a fat lip and an attitude to match landed me in the personnel office, being given two weeks' notice of termination of employment, which I didn't have to serve; I was asked to leave the premises immediately. Coincidently, Brendan got the sack from his job on the same day, so it was a double whammy when we informed Mum that evening.

At sweet sixteen I concluded that committed work was for other people. I would only take on work when I needed to, as I could also make money in other ways; my social life had to come first.

This wasn't the first time that I had gone to work or even home with my face rearranged by the odd fist, but the repercussions this time for those persons responsible for me getting the sack from my job were going to be a little bit extreme.

It happened on a typical Friday night. The pubs had just closed and I was walking home through the town centre with Eddie, Cockle, Morris and a couple of others. As we passed near the central park bus stops, I noticed a group of attractive girls, so I instinctively stopped to flirt with them. The fact that they were with their boyfriends was irrelevant to me, but what I didn't realise was that my friends had carried on walking, not noticing that I was no longer with them. This group of lads were from another town and were often the cause of many fights in our local pubs. Needless to say, I irritated them to the point of being punched out into the road by one of them and the rest of them joining in, 'laying in the boot', trying to kick me senseless as I lay on the tarmac drunk and confused.

By the time I got myself together, Morris had appeared. He came running onto the scene and dragged me away to catch up with the others.

"What the hell?" was my reaction to the others.

"We didn't even notice you weren't with us," they replied.

I was in such a state that they decided it best that they all just walked me home.

The next day I stayed in as long as I could, because I just looked a mess; then in the evening I went down to the 'Sally' to start my usual drinking binge. As I entered the pub, everyone was looking at me and commenting. Morris and a few of the others knew of the group that had 'jumped' me, and apparently I wasn't the first person to get a kicking from them; so we planned to put a stop to these lads picking us off.

The following Saturday we were ready. We set off on a pub crawl, gathering a crowd to meet up by the bus stops. We knew what pub the rival lads would come from and roughly how many of them there would be: no more than fifteen. By the time we reached the town centre, we had grouped to more than forty, aged from sixteen to mid-twenties.

We used to call our hometown the 'Village' as it seemed that everyone knew everyone, and as news got out, the crowd just kept growing. It seems that I must have been more popular than I thought, as we gathered skinheads, punks, souls boys, rockabillies – the whole town was rallying to my support.

The mood was set by Johnson, a friend of mine from the estate. As we neared the bus stops, a policeman approached us and shouted, "What are you up to, Johnson?" He was Johnson's uncle and was keen to disperse our growing crowd. Johnson surprised us all by decking his uncle policeman right there on the spot, with one well-aimed punch to the jaw.

We entered the town square where the bus stops and the central park were. I then directed all the different groups to separate, skinhead with skinhead, punk with punk, and so on, so that they would all look autonomous from each other. I offered to start the fight once the opposition turned up, as I would recognise the lad who started on me.

Eventually they entered the square, so, once again appearing alone, I walked over to them to start things off – but this time even my backup had backup!

I made the mistake of being too confident. As I approached the lad who had laid the first punch on me, I failed to notice his mate walking up beside me. As I focussed on the ringleader, I was suddenly knocked off guard by the mate's fist landing on my right cheek. Although I was knocked to the ground, my awareness levels were this time well-tuned. As I expected, he came towards me hoping to get a kick to my body, which made it easy for me to grab both his legs near his knees and push him off balance, making him fall backwards onto the ground. As he crashed back onto the road, I was instantly on top of him ready to punch down into his face, when I was suddenly rugby-tackled away from him.

This time, though, it was another friend of mine intervening. Robert, an old acquaintance, pulled me away from the fight scene, then said, "You've done enough; all you need to do now is watch and enjoy."

There were easily over sixty of us by now dispersed all over that town square. Simultaneously the others all moved together to become one group with the sole purpose of ending these outsiders. The violence reached such a crescendo that the only intervention from the police was to seal off the streets so that no traffic or innocent parties would end up in the middle of this small riot. Amazingly, although there were many casualties, with the police included, no arrests were made, even though two lads from the other gang ended up hospitalised for a while. The icing on the cake was that after a few weeks passed and things settled down a bit, I ended up becoming good friends with that rival gang and we ended up partying together and truly sharing girlfriends.

Brendan had made some others friends as well since buying his motorbike. I knew a few of them but chose to dislike them for no particular reason. Typically, one Saturday afternoon I came home to find his new biker mates all sitting in our front room; my mum had gone away for the weekend. I was in a strange mood so told them all to clear off, but they all ignored me – well, I was two years younger than all of them. Brendan told me to shut up and leave his mates alone, so I disappeared for a bit into my bedroom and planned to *make* them leave. I found my old air rifle and, after cocking it, I filled it with birdseed. Appearing back in the front room with my armed rifle, I told them to clear off again.

Harley, their 'leader', laughed at me and said, "What you gonna do? Shoot us if we don't?"

I walked over to him pointed the gun in his face and began to count. "One, two..."

"You wouldn't dare!" said Harley.

"Three..." *Pop!* Instantly, on the third count I pulled the trigger, shooting hundreds of tiny sharp seeds into Harley's face.

Harley flung himself back and put his hands over his face.

"Argh, are you mad?" he screamed.

I laughed out loud and then said, "Who's next?"

Instantly Brendan and his mates got up and left as I stood there laughing.

"Stupid Mad Dog!" one of them commented as they walked off into the hall.

Brendan, being the last to leave, stopped and turned to me saying, "You'd better clean all that mess up then, before Mother gets home."

Still laughing, I answered him, "I'll just tell her the budgie threw a party."

Feeling jealous of Brendan's freedom of movement with his motorbike, I managed to buy a moped, and for a short while I too enjoyed the freedom it brought. But within weeks of owning it, an unfortunate incident occurred. Late one night, after arriving home from the pub, I wasn't ready to call an end to the evening. Although I was very drunk, I thought it would be a good idea to go for a ride. My moped was quite fast and could reach a top speed of fifty miles per hour, so while cruising through the town centre, I decided to open her up and fly past one of my old local pubs. Then I tried to negotiate a turning just past the pub, but I miscalculated and put the bike into a bounce. Suddenly the front wheel span out of my control and I was flying over the handlebars, then landed with a thud as I continued to slide and roll on the tarmac road surface.

I was badly hurt, so I just lay motionless for a few seconds to assess how much I had damaged myself. I then looked up to see a crowd gathered all around me.

"Don't touch him! Call an ambulance!" I heard some bloke say.

Aww, crap! I'm drunk; if they call an ambulance the police will come too and I'll be nicked, I thought to myself. I decided to get up, and finally convinced everyone that I was fine and didn't need an ambulance. It was hard to get rid of the crowd, but eventually, after two helpful blokes had lifted my bike out of the road and placed it on the path, I sufficiently assured everyone that I was fine. I only lived less than a five-minute walk from the accident scene and walked off, shouting back to the stragglers who watched me walk away that I was fine. Once I had turned a corner and was out of sight, I sat on a short wall and winced with the pain that was shooting all through my body.

Eventually I got home and was greeted by Brendan saying, "What on earth has happened to you?"

"Smashed me bike up," I answered

After I explained what had happened, Brendan ran out to find my bike and wheeled it home, but it was beyond repair. I had a few sprains, grazes and bruises, but apart from shredding up my new jacket and trousers, plus losing my moped, I was generally okay. At sweet sixteen I began to think of myself as immortal and became increasingly convinced of this.

Around this time a few of my friends, Cockle included, had joined a government scheme to help the long-term unemployed retrain for employment – the 'Community Programme'. They encouraged me to get on board with them as you kept all your unemployment benefits and the work was really easy. The best part of this programme was that I knew most of the people on it and they were all having a great laugh and getting very stoned while working. At last I had found a job that suited my social life, so after a short interview I was accepted on the community programme with Brendan joining me a couple of weeks later.

The skills that I had learned from my grandad held me in good stead with all the supervisors, and I was often trusted to work alone which I sometimes enjoyed. But from day one, Cockle, Bren and I would turn up on time but be very stoned from start to finish. Amazingly we always got the jobs done, but the goings on were ridiculous; we would bring to work as much drug paraphernalia as we could and cause incidents everywhere.

I had a couple of accidents which I came away from totally unscathed, adding to my feeling of being immortal. Both were under the supervision of a bloke we named Sammy McKlegg. He was okay but greeted us every morning with a regular "Morning, each!" which annoyed us all intensely.

The first incident was while I was renovating the inside of an old church building. I'd set up my own scaffolding to reach the high ceiling beams but had ran out of short scaffold boards to stand on, so I substituted them with longer-sized boards that overshot the scaffolding. Sammy told me not to, saying that I had created a fall hazard. "Don't worry, I'll remember; plus, I'm the only one up here so I'll bar the overhang and be safe," I assured him.

Sure enough, I forgot and walked out on the large planks only to find myself suddenly falling over twenty feet towards the floor. The fall seemed to happen in slow motion; I could feel the sensation of air whizzing through me, while watching a desperate Sammy running in my direction. I landed catlike on all fours, totally unhurt, and began to stand upright while assuring the overconcerned Sammy that I was fine. I watched Sammy waving his arms around shouting something again and again, to which I was answering, "I'm fine!"

Then – *boing!* – something bounced off my head, knocking me again to the floor. After briefly falling on my knees, I stood back up to witness Sammy's shouts of concern turn to raucous laughter. I then realised what he had been shouting before: "The board, the board!" Unbeknown to me the scaffold board had flipped right over, somersaulted in mid-air and landed flat on my unprotected head as I rose from the ground to meet it.

As Sammy composed himself he asked me again if I was okay.

"Yes, I'm fine," I answered him. I'm not sure who was more surprised – me or him – that I wasn't hurt.

While working on another project, my colleague was on the roof of a three-storey historic building restacking a tall chimney. I was standing just under a triple extension ladder near the front door entrance. Sammy, being inside the building, walked towards me, then stopped and went very pale.

"Are you okay?" he suddenly asked.

"Yeah, I'm fine. Why?" I replied.

"Did you not just feel something hit your head?" He looked extremely puzzled.

"Yeah, I did. I felt something brush down my head and roll off my shoulder. What was it?" I asked, patting my head to where I had felt it, as I never did wear any of the supplied protective gear.

"A *brick!*" was Sammy's cold reply. "You should be dead!"

"Thanks, mate," I laughed back.

Sammy joined us outside and looked up at the height of the roof, then he looked at me, shook his head and walked off.

More and more, I began to think I was immortal, especially after a further incident at the travelling fairground.

On the occasional weekend, I would work on the fair with an old friend Leon, after a day of working on various rides. Chatting up girls and making a bit of cash, we got together with our friend Reggie who owned a few of the rides and set about dismantling the machinery ready to move on. The three of us were perched on stepladders while breaking down one of the rides. We started on a huge metal column that supported a moving three-seater hanging chair, Leon unbolting one end while Reggie did the other. I stood in the middle ready to help take the weight once it was completely freed. Just as they finished unbolting the column from the rest of the machinery, Leon's ladder collapsed, causing him to fall to the ground and roll out of the way. Instantly, Reggie jumped off from his ladder, getting clear from the heavy metal part that I was left holding on my own. I just stood there, perched on top of a freestanding stepladder holding a metal column that was about fifteen feet wide. The column was so heavy that it takes at least three people to systematically lower it to the ground, but I had the whole thing balanced in the palm of my hands.

Reggie, who was about six-foot-four and built like a tank, looked up at me from a safe distance so as not to get crushed by this machine part, and asked me, "How are you doing that? Are you Superman or something?"

I just kept extremely still, balancing on the top of a stepladder with the whole part in my hands and answered, "I haven't got a clue, but could you and Leon get up your bloody ladders and help me get this thing down?"

I was just as amazed as they were. I couldn't even feel the weight of this column, plus I am the clumsiest person I know, so how was I balancing this quarter of a ton lump of iron? Soon enough we lowered the heavy lump onto the floor, then after dismantling the whole ride decided we needed a drink. Every now and then during the rest of the evening we would try to explain what happened, but honestly I was just as confused as them.

When I think about these events, I am sure that even before I came to know Christ as my saviour, he had time and again sent angels to protect me and deliver me from calamity, although I can find no reason for me to deserve this protection. I was not in any way a nice bloke, as two of my colleagues on the community programme found out...

One of them interrupted a conversation I was having with Cockle. "Are you gonna do any work or just chat all day?" he called out one frosty morning across the field we stood in.

At the time, I was leaning on a shovel while talking and joking with Cockle. Without thinking, my reflex to this interruption was to throw with as much force as I could muster my shovel straight at him. The shovel flew spear-like, heading straight at his face. I felt myself tense up as the blade of it brushed passed his cheek, missing him by sheer millimetres.

"Ouch!" Cockle murmured as he stood in shock watching the event unfold.

Although I felt relieved at not having taken his face off literally, I then shouted abuse at him, warning him not to interrupt me again with his opinions and just get on with what he was there to do. He quietly went about his work at double pace and left Cockle and me to carry on our conversation.

On another site, I became the target of a huge bloke called Alfie. I had seen him around for years and knew him slightly. He was about six foot tall and rather fat, twice the size of me. After tolerating his jibes for a couple of days, I decided enough was enough.

Next morning, as we got our gear on, he put his feet into his welly boots and suddenly moaned saying, "Why are my boots wet? They are full of water!"

In front of everyone, I turned to him and said, "That's because I peed in them last night. You got a problem with that?"

Everyone started laughing at him, and I got ready for any repercussion he might throw at me. Instead, he just stood there and started to cry. I felt slight remorse and pity for this fellow, but then just told him not to start anything he can't follow through on. After the intervention from one of the supervisors, Alfie was moved to another site, but he didn't last much longer and left the community programme altogether.

But whatever confidence I had in myself was soon about to meet with my mortality. My attention was going to shift to a desire to know what life means and why it all seemed so pointless.

One typical Saturday afternoon, after a leisurely morning, I popped down to the local corner shop to get a packet of cigarettes. As I walked home I began to feel extremely fatigued. By the time I was about halfway home, I could hardly move my legs; they somehow felt detached. Every time I tried to walk as normal, putting one leg in front of the other, I was becoming less and less coordinated. My feet felt like they were just flapping and slapping onto the pavement bellow me. Eventually I just had to sit on a neighbour's wall and try to compose myself. *What the hell is wrong with me?* I thought while punching my legs to wake them up.

I sat there for over twenty minutes before gathering the ability to walk home. Eventually these weird symptoms seemed to pass – but only temporarily. Over the next few weeks I began to lose my strength periodically and was unable to recover. I could no longer attend work on the community programme, my appetite disappeared and I could only just get around with the aid of a walking stick. I had occasionally suffered with mild bouts of psoriasis but now it flared up all over my body. My weight quickly dropped and I went down to just eight stone. I could no longer face food but my appetite for alcohol stayed intact. I would need lifts to and from the pubs but occasionally would feel so exhausted I just had to get home almost immediately after arriving. It became normal for me to stay awake all night scratching my skin all over to try to appease the intense itching; my sheets would be covered in patches of blood where I had scratched away my skin. Then I would spend the day in a constant anxiety trying to gain relief, but now my hands were beginning to feel as dull as my legs. I also felt electrical discharges pulsate through my body into my fingers.

My doctor had prescribed me tranquilisers to help me sleep and referred me to the local hospital for tests, as he was at a loss as to what my condition was. Just to pass the time, I would take the tablets and drink as much beer as I could, hoping to pass out into oblivion. Eventually, after a host of tests including X-rays and scans, I was questioned by one of the hospital doctors.

"It's apparent that your reflexes aren't working and for some reason your nerves are not responding as they should. Just for the record, how much alcohol do you drink a week?" he asked.

I didn't want to tell him the full extent of my drinking, so what I told him was less than half the true amount.

"You are consuming way too much. Do you take drugs as well?" he continued.

"I smoke marijuana," I answered tentatively, hoping to avoid a further interrogation of my drug usage.

"Hmm... No, that wouldn't cause nerve damage like this, but your drinking must be at least halved. You are killing your nerves, or at least adding to what's going on," he exclaimed.

I knew I had to change my lifestyle but the thought of living without some sort of intoxication was an unbearable thought, so I resolved to drink less but smoke more dope. After a while my skin condition eased and, but for the odd spot, I was at peace. Slowly, too, the constant numbness in my arms and legs subsided. My appetite and strength increased, and after just over a year of being consumed with a mystery physical breakdown, my body was near on back to normal.

My thoughts, though, had grown very dark. I was convinced that death was very close to me and I had not gained enough of an understanding of what life was supposed to be about. Then I met *her* – Cybele. Apparently we had got together at a party a while before, but there had been so many girls during many a drunken binge that I could not place her at all. But she fascinated me. Her confidence and grasp of life took all my attention; she seemed to have all the answers I needed to hear, but the path she walked was darker than anything I could have ever imagined, so blindly I began to follow her into whatever abyss lay ahead.

CHAPTER NINE

The Darker Road

When I first met Cybele, I was hardly attracted to her; to me she seemed fairly plain. Most of my girlfriends were stunning in comparison, but there was something magnetic about her. She was quickly transitioning from being just an acquaintance that I occasionally met to an obsession whom I couldn't shake out of my thoughts.

Even though my life had now resumed to its old intensity of 'good times', although now more fuelled by drugs than alcohol, I found myself increasingly moving in the same circles as Cybele.

Cockle and I had linked up with quite a few drug suppliers, so getting stoned worked out far cheaper and accessible than drinking. Both Cockle and I soon developed our own delivery round, which meant I could smoke as much puff as I wanted with relatively no expense. But every now and then I would get what I describe as 'moments of clarity'.

On one such occasion I was standing outside a top floor flat in Walworth, London. I was the doorman, the lookout, the first person of contact if anything went down badly. Suddenly I found myself asking: *How did I get here? What have I become? Worse, what am I becoming? What decisions did I make to end up here and is there any going back?* Cockle was inside finishing off the final details of a deal which ended up with us bringing home around thirty ounces of cannabis resin in carrier bags on public transport.

During another deal where our suppliers were part time mercenaries, paid soldiers, hired killers, I questioned myself how or why I got on so well with these people. This meeting could have gone so very, very wrong, as we were interrupted by a complete stranger accusing me of being a police officer.

"I know him; he's a copper. I've seen him before; he's a fed, I'm telling you!" he shouted, pointing directly at me while telling the others what police station I was supposedly based at, which was coincidently Dartford, my hometown.

Things were growing very intense at this point until I started laughing, then said, "I know who you are talking about, you idiot. His name is Giles. Yeah, he looks like me – quite a few people have told me about my 'police double' – but I've grown up with most of these people here and I suggest you grow a brain and shut up!"

Cockle and the rest of my known group started laughing at this stranger, backing me up, stating you couldn't meet anyone who was further away from the police than me. The deal ended well and we started to bring in a lot of LSD into our home district.

I took a real liking to the psychedelic drugs, and Cybele had a few good contacts in the West Country for 'acid' and 'magic mushrooms'. She suggested that I should a take a trip with her to Dorset to meet with her brother and some other good friends of hers, especially as it was near mushroom harvest season.

By now Cybele had confided in me regarding her involvement in the occult and white magic. I had, with her help, begun to experience a spiritual awakening, with more than a few unexplainable events. I was developing a few weird abilities, which disturbed a few of my close friends. I began to read Tarot cards and practise astral projection, and could project thoughts into others so that they would hear my voice directly in their heads. On one occasion I did this to Cockle, as I needed to catch his attention when I saw him a distance away. He completely freaked out and threatened to cave my head in if I ever did it to him again. I was intrigued and transfixed by an alternate reality that seemed to give me some of the answers I had been looking for since my disillusioned childhood.

This weekend in Dorset with Cybele excited me to my inner being, not just because of the drugs but also because I envisaged a closer walk in the magic realm. I was avidly reading one of the books that she had lent me called *The Ultimate Book on the Occult*, and I knew she could teach me so much more. I was not disappointed.

Her brother Greg was a 'cool dude' and clearly respected by his large friendship group that regularly gathered around his house. The weekend was spent getting very stoned and tripping out on an avid supply of 'magic mushrooms'. Greg was a bit of an artist and his house was furnished throughout with murals that he had painted on the walls. One such mural that comes to mind was of a large skeleton rolling a spliff; underneath was written, "We are the people our parents warned us about." I had to laugh when I saw it. "How true!" I commented.

During this weekend Cybele explained to me how she was initiated into a coven. She went into great detail to explain to me how the priest and priestess showed her that she was loved and warmly invited her to become one of them. Their first words to her when she was introduced were, "Human, come join us." She then turned to me and said, "They want to meet you, Glenn. Satan loves you and wants you, but you're not ready yet." She then instantly closed off and ignored me for the rest of the weekend and we had a very silent and awkward journey home, leaving me wondering what I had done wrong and left hanging with desire, wanting the answers that I knew only she could give.

As the next few weeks rolled by, Cybele opened up again and told me about some of the other people that she knew who were into witchcraft. I was surprised at who they were and how many of them there were. Some of these people were old friends of mine, and I had spent many an evening at various places getting very stoned with them. I also became very aware that Cybele seemed to have quite a few young men under her spell wherever we went, including in Dorset; she often boasted to me how madly in love with her they all were. One close friend of mine, 'Mufty', only had two obsessions in his life: heroin and Cybele. Even though I was dating his sister, he constantly accused me of having an affair with Cybele. I could see why; I was now always in her company. I questioned myself over and over whether I had become yet another lapdog to her, but assured myself that I was just using her to gain knowledge. I also became very aware of a trail of destruction for those who were close to her, but put it down to coincidence, even though I had witnessed Mufty's life deteriorate out of control as he had become consumed by his heroin addiction.

A while previously, during the time when I was going through my weird illness, I went to a strip show set up at a local football club house. I was chatting there to an acquaintance called Nigel – a loud character with a notorious reputation around the local estate. Although I hardly knew him, he constantly went on about a new love of his life. He was so stricken with her that he had just left his wife and family for this girl. She was called Cybele, and he went on and on about her, asking if I knew her. At that time I only knew her vaguely and could not see why he was so obsessed. I later found out that just a few weeks after that conversation he died of a drug overdose while camping with her at the Glastonbury festival.

Whenever I questioned in my mind my involvement with her, Cybele would turn up at my house, telling me how fond she was of me and that we had something special together. She would then always say reassuringly, "I'm not evil, Glenn. I'm not evil and you will be mine." Sadly, I was beginning to think that being hers was not such a bad thing.

I ended up getting a job with her, working at a local psychiatric hospital as a domestic. Most of our colleagues thought that we were brother and sister, as by now we had grown very close and spent all our spare time together. "You both have that same look in your eyes," many of them would comment. It also didn't take long for me to develop another source of income by providing drugs to a surprising number of the staff there. Mufty's sister Mish, my girlfriend, also joined us on staff, although I really liked her and found her extremely attractive. I just couldn't fight the need to be around Cybele, something that Mish seemed absolutely fine with, which was weird to say the least.

Cybele introduced me to a couple of spiritualists who worked with us, and I became intrigued by their understanding of the spirit world, especially when they invited us to join them at the Christian spiritualist church to listen to a visiting medium.

Later that same week I was called into my new manager's office and was very surprised to discover the reason why. As I entered her office she suddenly blurted out, "I hear you are thinking about going to listen to a medium. Don't do it! Please, it's so dangerous and satanic. I used to be a medium and needed an exorcism to get away from it. I then got cancer and I am sure it was linked to my involvement in that horrible, dark demonic craft. If you go, bad things will happen!"

I just stood there thinking, *what a weirdo!* Then I answered, "Err, okay, but these people are *Christian* spiritualists. They sing hymns and all that, so it's harmless. I'm just going to find out more of what it's all about."

She then went on about how there can be no such thing as a 'Christian' spiritualist – that the two things are a complete contradiction. She also quoted the Bible and continued trying to convince me. I did my best to ignore her while pretending to listen.

Later that day Cybele asked me what the manager was talking to me about so I told her. She laughed and then said with a venom in her tone,

"Stupid cow! Those Bible-bashers don't have a clue. We really ought to just mess her head up."

"Yeah," I answered as, not for the first time, I saw a very dark and chilling side of Cybele's character.

Friday night soon came about and Cybele called round for me at seven o'clock prompt. "Hurry up! We don't want to be late. The thing starts at seven thirty. We want good seats," she said

I just had to put my jacket on and then I was ready to leave. It was only about a ten-minute walk to the spiritualist church from my house, so off we set – Cybele, her friend Sally and I.

I felt huge waves of apprehension pass through me as we got ready to enter through the church doors. Mainly due to my insistence, we sat right at the back, and I felt quite hidden by the rows of people in front of me.

As I peered around the church hall, I was intrigued to see a group of people that Cybele had revealed to me were into witchcraft. *Why on earth would they come to a church service?*

The service started with a welcome, followed by a time of singing hymns, just like I had experienced in my Catholic childhood days at Christmas. Then after a short while we were invited to sit, and the visiting medium took control of the meeting. Suddenly the old panic began to consume my mind: feelings of 'who am I' and 'where did I begin' started to flood into my thoughts. They were closely followed by what I call 'internal thought Tourette syndrome'. I sunk as low as I could, trying to hide in the back row as a barrage of offensive insults consumed my mind, all aimed towards the medium. I just wanted to jump up and leave the hall.

Then my worst fear was realised: her eyes connected with mine. No longer did I feel invisible or hidden, but instead totally exposed.

"You, at the back... yes, you, young man... please stand up!" she called out.

Reluctantly, I rose slowly to my feet, whilst the insults in my mind still raged against her.

"I have a message from a small man to give you," she said. "He is very short – under five foot – and was very close to you in life." She then continued to give an avid description of my grandad.

"Do you know someone like that?" she then enquired.

"Yes, my grandad," I admitted, but I thought, *Woman, you have got something very wrong.*

"Yes, he is your grandad and he knows your life is in a real state of flux at the moment," she went on.

"Hang on... Before you continue, my grandad is still alive! You described him well but you are wrong," I declared, thinking, *Got you! You're just one big fake.*

But to my amazement she just carried on. "No, not your grandad, but another relative close to him, anyway."

She then went on to describe many things that were going on in my life: the confusion, the fear, that I was going through an intense period of searching for something real. Then she moved from generalising to describing some very fine points in my life, which I found very disturbing.

"Finally you are entering a new relationship and you are questioning trust. Just let go and trust," she concluded. Then she pointed directly at me and said sternly, "You will come back to this church!" The way she said this and the tone she used struck a deep chord internally. She reminded me of Cybele – the way she was always saying, "I will have you."

Cybele then turned to me and said, "You're falling in love with me. Ha, you can't stop it! I've put a spell on you; you will be mine."

Confusion filled my mind. I turned to Cybele and she appeared to be glowing. As I looked at her, it felt like my mind was being reprogrammed. The only way I can I describe it was like my mind was reeling back and forth with images of everyone I had loved, and over their images pictures of Cybele were being superimposed. I winced as I tried to shake it all off; part of me was always repulsed by her. In reality I felt like I actually didn't even like her, but I was also strongly drawn like a moth to the flames to give in to what was happening.

"We have been together in all eternity. Past lives confuse with this one," she whispered to me.

"Stuff this, I'm off!" I said.

I stood up and left as fast as I could, with Cybele and Sally following me through the exit. As I hurriedly directed our departure towards the comfort of a favourite pub, Cybele skipped and danced to Sally, singing, "Glenn Walsh loves me! Glenn Walsh loves me! Told you he would! Ha ha! Told you it still works!"

"Shut up, you stupid girl," I answered. "I'm meeting Mish down at the Oak. You're not even my type," but inside I felt I was losing whatever defences I had put up to resist her grip on my life.

CHAPTER TEN

Bad Things Will Happen

After that crazy medium experience, I decided to put a bit of space between Cybele and myself, so I spent the next two evenings with Mish. But sure enough, as soon as I was back at work, Cybele would not shut up about it; nor did my manager, as the first thing she asked was whether I had gone to that spiritualist church.

"We prayed you wouldn't go," she said while looking very disappointed that I had ignored her warning.

Later I laughingly explained the conversation to Cybele saying, "Obviously her prayers don't work."

The following Wednesday evening I was relaxing, watching television, when my mum interrupted, telling me to carry a three-foot-long empty fish tank that I had left sitting in the conservatory into the garage. After I endured her nagging for a short while, I was stirred to move and said, "Okay, okay, give me a moment."

She left through the front door and walked around to the garage block situated at the end of our row of terraced houses. I followed a few seconds behind her carrying the large glass tank.

I stopped near the garage as she struggled to open the large up-and-over door, then as I struggled with the tank walking towards the garage, I became overwhelmed by confusion. I struggled to hold my footing and stop myself walking in a daze. My mind streamed with what I can only describe as 'windblown voices', but I couldn't understand what they were saying.

Then I realised I was heading towards a small brick wall with a four-foot drop the other side. I was aware of it so I tried hard to stop my moving forward, but before I knew it my legs hit the wall and I was falling over it with the tank still in my hands. As I tipped over, I lost my grip and the glass tank hit the floor beneath me, shattering all four sides from the top downwards, leaving long dagger-like strands of glass standing upright as they remained glued to the unbroken bottom of the tank.

I could hear my mum scream. Once again everything seemed to go in slow motion: I was looking down onto the glass shafts which were waiting to receive my falling body, when instinct took over, so while automatically placing both arms out to brace my fall, I felt my left hand grab a shaft. The glass slid into my hand like a hot knife going through butter. Fortunately my right hand hit the floor and broke my fall, and with both arms extended I stopped my upper torso from being pierced by the glass daggers. Then I slowly and nervously rose to my feet, pulling my hand free from the glass shaft. After feeling the glass slide from deep within my hand, blood began to pump out of a gaping hole that I tried in vain to close up with my right hand by grasping the wound tightly.

"I had visions of your head being cut off. I could see your head rolling off. What happened? Why did you have to leave that tank sitting there for weeks?" my mum started shouting hysterically.

"Just take me to the hospital, will you, or I'll to run up there myself!" I shouted, interrupting her ranting.

Within half an hour I was sitting in West Hill Hospital A & E (known then as Casualty) looking at what had the appearance of raw liver hanging open from my palm, watching my blood shoot out in rhythm with my heartbeat. A nurse immediately made me hold my hand above my heart and keep pressure on the wound. I was quickly taken into a room and my hand was being injected with stuff supposedly to ease the pain, but to be honest all they did was made it hurt all the more.

"Stop digging me," I blurted out as one of the medical staff lifted open my flap of flesh then stuck a needle deep into the wound. My mum nearly passed out as she tried to observe.

Then just moments later, while having my hand stitched up and being warned that there was a good chance that I could lose the use of my left hand, I couldn't help thinking of the warning my manager had given me: "Bad things will happen!" I felt very confused and unsafe as I tried to explain how I had come to fall. I couldn't tell the medical staff or even my own mother that I felt I had been pushed by an imagined invisible force, so I just said, "I didn't see the wall," but even that didn't explain how the tank shattered in an unusual manner; glass just doesn't break like that.

The pain relief that I was given had little to no effect on me even after a shot of pethidine, so as soon as I got out of the hospital, I said goodbye and thanks to my mum and headed to Cybele's to get stronger relief by chasing heroin.

As we smoked the heroin, I related the events to Cybele. Eventually, when the heroin brought me the relief that I was seeking, I began to open up to her about reoccurring nightmares I had had as a child, things that I had seen in my room, including a large, black dog with piercing, red eyes.

I still remember well the reoccurring dream that haunted me for months when I was around six years old. Every night as I slept, I found myself walking down a dark forest road. I felt afraid, knowing something was after me. Then I would hear the sound of galloping hooves, the crack of a whip and the noise of wooden carriage wheels tearing up the ground as they sped towards me. Next, through the moonlit sky, I could see his silhouette charging towards me, the dark man in the top hat, driving the horse and carriage directly at me. Frozen by fear, I stood watching as the giant beasts dragged the carriage closer and closer until I could see his eyes staring out of the darkness full of hatred straight at me. "Mine!" he would always shout just as they descended down upon my small frame, instantly waking me to a sheer terror-driven flight into my parents' bedroom.

Then one night during this same dream, for a reason still unknown to me, I decided it was time to stop him. I stood frozen by fear just as the dream always played out, with him closing in on me, but as his gazing stare broke out through the darkness, I stood my ground, pointed directly at him, and with all the boldness that I could muster shouted at him, "Stop! This is just a dream and you cannot hurt me!" Immediately I woke and for a change felt at peace rather than fearful and was never haunted by that dream again.

"Sounds to me like you are being chased by death," Cybele said in conclusion to her interpretation of what I had relayed.

"I'm glad he's a slow runner then," I laughed as the intoxicating effects of the heroin purged through my mind, relaxing me to an uncaring state of pure lethargy.

Two evenings later, with my hand stitched and bandaged up and placed in a sling to keep it above my heart, I found myself at a party with Cockle and Cybele, in the psychiatric hospital that Cybele and I worked at. As the evening wore on, the drug supply diminished rapidly, so Cockle and I decided to go and get some more. We drove to an old friend's flat on the Temple Hill estate, knowing that he had just got in a good supply of 'bush'.

It was around ten at night when we parked the car and walked around to Dingo's flat. As we walked, there was a large gang of around twenty young men hanging around outside. They all stood in our way trying to stare us out, but we just ploughed through the middle of them, walking directly to the front door. Karen, who was Dingo's pregnant girlfriend, opened the door to let us in, as Dingo was out but due back anytime soon. Both Cockle and I followed her into the front room, ready to skin up and wait for Dingo's return. Karen left the room to put the kettle on and make tea for us, when suddenly we heard a loud bang as the front door came flying open. Streams of balaclava-hooded men came flooding into the flat armed with various weapons. I watched in shock as the heavily pregnant Karen was punched straight in the face and flew backwards into her settee, which fortunately broke her fall.

Cockle jumped up to defend her but was hit around the face with a cosh by another assailant, knocking him into the wall. I quickly rushed toward him to fight off the group that had gathered around him, although realising that I only had one hand to fight with as my left was still strapped to my chest.

Then I heard an overwhelming *crack!* I glanced over to my right, only to see the fireplace coming towards me. For a brief second I thought, *What is going on?* Then there was blackness.

One of the gang had gone behind me and hit me around the back of the head with a set on nun chucks, splitting my head open and knocking me unconscious. Shortly after, I came around to see someone perched on an armchair, pointing a gun in my direction. Fortunately it was Dingo.

"Glenn, I didn't realise it was you. I couldn't recognise you with all that 'claret' over your face. You'd better get that head stitched up soon. You're bleeding out, mate," he said as I slowly turned towards him to see what was going on.

As quickly as the gang had crashed in on us they had fled. Apparently they didn't know who we were, but once one of them realised, they wanted to get away as soon as possible, especially as Dingo's dad was a notorious gypsy who was very well known for dishing out violence.

During the next few weeks, the 'Ferret', Dingo's dad, shattered a few kneecaps as he traced his way through this gang's ringleaders.[5]

Again, within just a couple of days of piercing my hand, I was being stitched up at the local hospital. And again I found myself pondering my manager's warning, "Bad things will happen."

The following weekend after the incident at Dingo's, a group of us headed down to Camber Sands. Freddy, one our good friends, owned a couple of houses situated right on the beach, so we spent many weekends 'chilling out' in our usual manner in this idyllic location. In walking distance of the beach was a pub that attracted the local Hell's Angels chapter, and although we had a few close disputes with them, we generally all got on well.

The night was going well; I had managed to 'pull' an attractive blonde called Paula who wanted to come back to the house with me to use my 'pipe' and smoke something a bit more 'hard core' later in the evening. After a while we realised that Freddy had gone missing, so I suggested that I'd go and look in the car park for him. It didn't take me long to find him; as soon as I walked out of the back door, I could see him propped backwards against a car with his head leaning back. Another bloke was standing directly in front of him with his arm stretched out. As I closed in on them, I realised why Freddy was standing so still: the other bloke has gone to stab him in the face, but as he struck out, the knife had jammed between Freddy's front teeth.

"Woah!" I called out as I closed in on them, holding my right arm out as a gesture to stop.

Although my left hand was no longer in a sling, it was still bandaged up and swollen to more than twice its usual size, plus it was extremely sore and throbbed like an abscessed tooth. I hid my left hand behind my back to give the appearance that I was holding a weapon. The stranger quickly pulled out the knife and turned to face me. Freddy then repositioned himself ready to take him on again.

---

[5] Recently, roughly thirty years after these events, I was in a pub with a group of church friends when a cousin of one of our group came up to me asking where I had grown up. "Dartford," I answered. "You're Glenn Walsh," he said. "I am. Do I know you?" I responded. He then went on to tell me that he was one of the balaclava-clad strangers and that after he had realised who we were, he had fled to Ireland the next day, staying there for nearly a year, hoping that things would soon blow over. We ended up having a good chat about the old days and with him coming along to church.

Again I called out, "Woah, stop! Look, mate, just disappear – and Freddy, get back in the pub."

Luckily the stranger turned and ran off. I had to stop Freddy going after him, then showed him my hand, reminding him that I would be a bit useless as backup.

Once again after this evening, which was yet another drug-fuelled night, I began to evaluate how crazy my life was becoming, and a huge desire to get away from it all grew within me. Bad things had always happened around me, but they seemed to be accelerating well beyond my control.

CHAPTER ELEVEN

Move and I'll Shoot

"Fancy moving to Bridport with me? We could stay with my friends, Chris and Paula; they have a big house with three spare bedrooms," Cybele asked me out of the blue.

"Funny that, I was thinking about getting away from all this crap somehow. A fresh start in the West Country might be what I need. Okay, you fix it up and I'll move down there with you," I answered.

I was surprised how quickly things worked, and before I knew it the move was imminent. I had a big send off with about thirty of my friends all meeting in the Bull & Vic pub to drop 'acid' and tour the town on a final LSD trip. As we dished out the 'acid', I felt like we were taking communion together just like in a Catholic setting, but this was far more enjoyable. Then within a few days, Cybele and I travelled down together and my new life in Dorset began. I was just nineteen years old and felt free to be whatever I wanted.

Things started well. I managed to find work in a local chip shop, which meant I ate well – free cod and chips every lunchtime. I could pay the small rent asked by Chris, and I had enough spare money to keep a good supply of drugs coming my way. Very quickly I began making the right connections, and the 'acid', 'mushrooms' and 'puff' began to dominate my daily routine. Before long I changed jobs, but as usual couldn't hold on to employment. I was also making a few enemies and began running up a few debts. I managed to upset one local character who was a county boxing champion and I heard that he was after me, so I decided to use a learnt occult practice to warn him away by sending him nightmares. It seemed to work effectively enough; when I encountered him with a few of his friends, he told me that we were okay, as he stood looking uncharacteristically awkward, and that I could let things go now.

As my finances dwindled and my hope of working out a life in Dorset looked less real, Cybele came up with a new idea. She knew of a couple of guys, Barry and Stig; they lived for free in a caravan sited at the edge of a chicken farm in the middle of nowhere. We could move in with them if we liked; with a few of our new links, we could exist on a few drug transactions and literally drop out of society altogether.

I had got to know these guys by tripping out with them a couple of times; they called themselves anarchists and were searching for an alternative lifestyle, which certainly appealed to me. So for a while, Stig, Barry, Cybele and I lived a remote lifestyle of getting as stoned as we liked, tripping out on LSD and exploring occult practices together.

Then one day, much like any other, we had gone off in the car to score some marijuana. This time the only stuff around was in a resin form, but it was potent enough. On the way back from the deal, Barry was giving a lift to an old friend of his whom we had met at the dealer's house. Barry drove and was having a heated discussion with this bloke. Suddenly he started hitting Barry and then turned to start on Stig, who was sitting behind Barry. Cybele sat between Stig and me, while I was seated behind this violent stranger.

Taking action, I leaned over between him and his passenger door, opened the door, grabbed him and managed to push him out of the moving vehicle. Unfortunately for him he was not wearing a seatbelt and rolled out into the side of the road. As we sped off, leaving him lying there, silence filled the car until Stig said, "Crap! That was Pauley Smith. He's a right handful and his gang will tear us up for that!"

Barry answered, "*If he's still alive.* That was a bit extreme, wasn't it, Glenn?"

I just answered, "He shouldn't have messed with my mates, then."

I had only known Stig and Barry for a relatively short time, so we were all still a bit unsure of each other.

We got back to the caravan and decided to get totally 'wasted' while Barry grew in his paranoia of how Pauley would get revenge.

"Calm down, guys. Does this Pauley know where we live? If he don't, no one could find us out here. Blimey, the farmer's house is nearly a mile away and the nearest neighbour at least five miles away."

We spent the rest of the day getting as stoned as possible. As the evening went on, we all got 'the munchies' so decided to venture down to the chicken houses and grab some eggs to eat. Although the caravan enjoyed a power source that gave us lighting, outside was pitch darkness.

There were no streetlights to be seen nor houses to illuminate the blackness; even the moonlight was obscured by the dense foliage of the trees that surrounded us. So into the dark without the possession of one torch among us, we ventured through the woods and the tumbling fields, following instinct as to where the chicken houses should be. Between us we must have collected in excess of forty eggs. After negotiating a near on hysterical journey back, while losing a few eggs along the way, we found our way to the still illuminated caravan.

As we stumbled our way back, I could hear noises coming from the woods behind me. I turned and tried to see, peering into the darkness.

"There's someone out there!" I said to the group.

"Now who's paranoid?" Barry answered.

But I could sense a presence in the woods. I felt that we were being watched by something or someone unseen.

"Pass me some more eggs!" I called to Stig, who then handed over about ten of them. One by one I threw them into the trees, aiming towards the sounds that I had heard and where I felt a presence.

"You sure Pauley don't know where we live," I shouted into the caravan, "cos I tell you, there's someone in the woods. Come out, come out, whoever you are!" I then called mockingly into the darkness.

Cybele, Stig and Barry were all adamant that I was just very stoned and very paranoid, and convinced me to join them in the caravan for yet another joint. After they had fried a few eggs, we all sat down to eat and drink some local cider.

Suddenly there was a loud bang on the door.

"Who the...?" we all shouted, jumping to our feet in readiness to meet whomever was out there.

Barry walked over to the door as we stood ready, thinking it must be Pauley come to take his retribution for the earlier scuffle. As Barry opened the door, his face went very pale and he silently and steadily walked backwards. Bursting through the door were six men dressed in camouflage clothing and pointing guns in our direction.

"Nobody move! Keep very, *very* still! Move and I'll shoot!" one of them was shouting.

They positioned themselves in the caravan so that each of us had at least one gun trained on our foreheads.

"I know you said Pauley was a handful, but this is a bit extreme!" I shouted at Barry

"Shut it!" the bloke with the gun in my face said.

After what seemed like a lifetime, but in reality could only have been a few seconds, the man who was doing the most shouting identified himself as police.

Phew! I thought to myself. It's amazing how rapidly thoughts can rush through your mind to bring you to a place of relative peacefulness. *It's only the police. We have hot-knifed most of our gear. If they had come a few hours earlier they could have got us all for dealing, but now if we all put our hands up to it, they only have enough to charge us with possession; that's around a £100 fine. It's cool.*

I relaxed.

Actually, we *all* seemed to relax spontaneously, which caused a bit of tension amongst the police. As they began to tear up the caravan, searching for whatever evidence they could use against us, one of them came in carrying Stig's guitar.

"What shall I play?" he asked mockingly, hoping to provoke us.

"How about 'Please release me, let me go', Tom Jones style?" I laughed back at him.

The power shift was quick. No longer were we intimidated by these gun-wielding strangers. Now the police were dealing with a group of social deviants who were stoned and unafraid.

Realising the situation, they quickly handcuffed Cybele and me together and forced us out, through the woods, across the field and into waiting police vehicles. They drove us for miles until we ended up in Weymouth Police Station. This was the early 1980s, and although I had known and deserved the rough end of police justice, I was running on overdrive. I kept shouting all kinds of jovial messages to my friends and laughing loudly as I shouted out of my cell, hoping to provoke the police authorities somehow.

Eventually I gave in to the boredom offered by this bleak cell and sat down to start counting the tiles on the wall – a little game I had invented for myself on the numerous occasions that I had been placed in police custody. After a while I noticed a small book at the end of the bed. I picked it up and looked it over. *Reader's Digest* was the front title. I flicked through it looking for something to take my interest; then I found a dramatic story which consumed all my attention until I realised it was about someone who had experienced a supernatural encounter with Jesus. I stopped reading, held the book up in the air, then threw it across the cell, slamming it into the wall.

"Jesus? I don't want to read any of this crap about Jesus!" I shouted.

I then looked up at the ceiling and mockingly shouted, "If you're up there, God, I don't want to know you. I don't want you in my life; stay away from me!" I continued on and on with the rant.

My anger against this God was like a volcanic eruption – until I heard the banging of doors. I then headed to the vent on my door and shouted out to the corridor, "I want my lawyer. His name is Perry Mason. If he's busy I want Bruce Wayne!" Once again I was laughing and mocking the police, then three of them came into my cell and instructed me to follow them to another room.

As we entered the room, a large man in a crinkly suit told me to sit down, then blurted out, "You had better stop laughing. We are about to interview you!"

"It's OK, mate. I don't want the job," was my response.

To say that my attitude wasn't very helpful and made this CID officer lose his temper would be an understatement, but I felt very satisfied that it had made some of the other officers chuckle.

I then went silent until they convinced me that they had enough evidence to charge me with something; I had learnt over the years not to admit to anything. Once they relayed what they had, and I knew it was enough to convict me, then I would say, "It's a fair cop; that will do," as my statement – as in this case, a charge of possession of cannabis. But that's as far as I would go. "You tell me what I've done; I won't tell you or confess to a thing," was my personal motto.

Three months later I was fined the sum of £100 through the local magistrate's court for possession of cannabis – yet another petty crime to add to my growing portfolio of convictions.

Our hidden life was over though. We now knew that we were being watched, and although the police had mistimed this operation, next time they could be more effective. After the court case, I decided to return back to Kent, and Mish was very keen to come down and collect me in her new car to take me home. Cybele had moved into her brother's house and decided to stay on in Bridport and couldn't believe that I would leave without her. Just before Mish arrived, I went to say goodbye to Cybele and once again felt very confused in her presence.

"You can't leave me. We are the same person, Glenn," she said as over the radio played 'Don't you forget about me' by Simple Minds.

Again I could see Cybele glow, childhood memories flashed through my mind and called out for her.

"Don't go," she repeated.

I shook my head to try to rid myself of the confusion. *Stupid song! Why now? Why now at this time is that song playing?* I strengthened my resolve and just said, "Bye, Cybele. Mish will be waiting for me so I'd better go." Then I turned and after two brief years in Bridport returned to Kent.

I had contacted Cockle about my return – and what a welcome I was getting! Coincidently, a few old friends were planning a trip to Jersey the very next day and of course invited me to join them. Rod's dad had a private plane and offered to fly us there, plus we could stay with Rod's uncle and aunt.

My mum was looking forward to seeing me but nearly cried at my appearance. "You look like a dropout tramp," were her welcoming words. I had to quickly rush to the bathroom and snort a line of powder before engaging her in conversation.

I had dinner with the family before heading down to the pub to meet up with Cockle and the others. I managed to smarten myself up a bit as I went to my old wardrobe; it was good to have my old bedroom back, as Brendan had moved in with a girlfriend.

As I walked into the town, I heard someone call out, "Walshy!" I turned to see who it was and had to laugh as I saw my old friend Derek, who while in the middle of punching someone to the ground shouted out to welcome me home.

"Just like old times!" I laughed over to him.

I met Cockle, Rod, Ade and Jerry in the Bull & Vic, and we all planned the trip to Jersey together. It felt good to be home. Next morning Rod picked me up in his Mercedes sports car and off we drove to Biggin Hill airport where his dad kept his plane. As soon as we caught up with Cockle and the others, we decided to get really stoned ready for the journey. Jerry had some exceptional cannabis that would rival 'skunk', which would set us up for our vacation.

What an adventure this was turning out to be: a private plane just for us, plus during the flight Rod's dad invited me take control of the wheel and guide us through the sky; the others were freaking out knowing just how stoned we all were, and I must admit when he told me to just head for the horizon I was a bit overwhelmed, picturing myself as a small dot in the sky. But we got there safely and soon settled in with Rod's family.

We spent the week relaxing on beaches, drinking and smoking, and met a group of girls to hang around with. One night everyone shot off early leaving me and Rod to drink on until the early morning hours. We didn't feel like walking far afterwards, so I asked him to choose a car to go home in. Rod looked at a sporty-looking black Ford.

"How about that one?" he suggested.

Within seconds I had the driver's door open, then had the engine started.

"Can I drive?" he asked.

"Of course!"

After driving around the island, we headed back and decided to leave the car in a random field about half a mile from the house. As we turned through an open gate into the field, we suddenly found ourselves driving on wooden pallets. We drove on a couple of hundred yards to hide the vehicle but then had to negotiate walking back over pallet after pallet, which, because of our intoxicated state, proved a lot harder than driving over them.

I was enjoying our holiday and trying to chill out and forget Cybele as much as possible. Then one night my peace was shattered. I was sharing a room with Ade who woke me as he nearly shouted, "Are you okay?"

"Why?" I questioned.

"You were crying out for help. Blimey, you sounded so desperate it scared the crap out of me!" he explained.

"I'll tell you in the morning over breakfast," I promised him.

Next morning, as Rod's aunt served us breakfast, I got her attention and then asked her outright, "Are you in some sort of coven?"

She looked a bit stunned but didn't answer yes or no. Instead she just questioned why I was asking.

At this point a disgruntled Cockle walked out of the dining room muttering, "I hate this freaky crap."

"I saw you in a dream last night. You and Bill were practising magic rituals and I was being drawn into something beyond my control," I said.

"Do you have a gift? I'd like to hear more from you later," she replied with a huge smile.

Rod later told me that his aunt and uncle had told him I was welcome to stay on longer once the week was over. Although it was a nice offer, the fear that I had experienced in my dream drove me to leave when the others did and fly home with them.

Once back home my life quickly resumed to exactly how it had been before the Bridport venture. I even found myself back on the community programme, stoned as usual.

One morning Cockle called around for me to walk to work with him, but I had a growing feeling I should just stay at home that day. "Just don't feel up to it today. Tell the bosses I'm sick," I said to him, then I just sat back to watch a bit of morning television.

I began to feel uneasy trapped in my own house – a bit stir-crazy but unable to leave. *What's wrong with me?* I couldn't concentrate on anything but once again I found myself thinking about Cybele. *No, I'm not going down that road again. I'm free of her.*

I began to sketch things just to fill my mind with anything but her, when suddenly the doorbell rang. *What now?* I thought to myself while walking towards the door.

Opening it, I couldn't believe who was standing there right in front of me.

"Hello, Glenn. I knew I'd find you in. I'm back! Aren't you going to welcome me in?" Cybele said.

"How? Why? I just knew I couldn't go out today. I couldn't get you off my mind today. *How?*" I blurted out, confused once again in her presence.

"Did you forget about me? I told you not to," she said as I made us a cup of tea.

We spent the next few hours chatting, but in my heart I vowed not to let myself come under her control again. However, as hard as I tried, I just could not keep her from consuming my thoughts. Within weeks of her coming back, I dumped Mish and then spent as much time with Cybele as I could. She told about the love spells that she cast using candles and by keeping articles of affection. Inside I lived in a perpetual state of contradiction: I hated and despised her but also had an overwhelming conviction that we were meant to be together and that only with her my life would make sense. If this was love, I hated it. The confusion increased, as did her hold over me; she would often speak out what was in my thoughts, and once turned to me as if to warn me when I had thoughts of getting away from her, saying, "Remember the itching..." Then another time I heard her laughing with her friend Sally saying, "It still works. He's still mine." Then she called out loud so that I would hear her mock me, saying, "He loves me! He loves me!" again and again.

CHAPTER TWELVE

Let the Battle Commence

We have reached the point at which my story began: that 'dreadful night' with Cybele, with the 'acid' trip of horrors; the shadow-like figure in the drive of the spiritualist church; the voice that commanded, "You will do my bidding"; the new voice of hope which said, "Everyone who calls on the name of the Lord will be saved"; and the battle that ensued within me. But God had heard my cry and there seemed to be a light at the end of this nightmarish tunnel. I had asked God for a sign and he had given it in the face of Jesus.

Now I thought about the other words that the voice bringing hope had spoken: "Knock and the door will be opened to you; for all who seek find and to anyone who knocks the door will be opened." *How then do I knock? How do I seek out who this Jesus is? Where do I begin?*

My life changed instantly, although mainly fuelled by a guilt-based panic. I stopped taking heavy drugs – no more heroin, no more LSD – although at that time in my life I didn't see marijuana as a problem to me.

I needed to make sure that the sign of the face of Jesus was real and not just a symptom of me being stoned, and that I was not suffering from some kind of psychosis. So I decided to go round to Barney's and photograph the door, just to make sure that it was still there – a real sign. Although I felt that my behaviour would seem idiotic to everyone else, with a camera in hand I knocked on Barney's door.

Barney invited me in and I wandered upstairs to his front room. He was having Sunday lunch with a couple of mutual friends. Embarrassed, I explained that I just wanted to photograph his living room door and would then depart quickly. The whole group watched me in an awkward silence as I stood in their front room taking a picture of a door.

"You OK?" Barney asked.

"Yeah, I just think this might be a bit special and I need to rush off. Sorry!" I answered.

I'd done it. The face was there. The wood grain was unusually formed to resemble the face of Jesus. It wasn't the drugs, it was real, and hopefully I'd captured it on film.

It's funny where we put our hope. My future seemed to depend on whether a living room door had a pattern of wood grain that to me resembled an image of what I believed Jesus looked like… But I had asked for a sign, for him to show me a way out, a way forward from my nightmare existence. This had to be so much more than coincidence – a homing beacon guiding me through a smog-filled confusion of reality.

Anxiously I waited for my photos to be developed, as this was well before the digital age. Then, when I collected them from the pharmacy, I couldn't wait to get home before I examined them.

Yes! There – I can see it on the photos! It is there, this is real! Jesus, you are my way to God! This is not just a huge psychotic episode.

From that day on I kept those photos close to me as a constant reminder to help me through the daily battle.

Still the evil thoughts raged, still the fear engulfed me, still what was real around me threatened to disappear and be replaced by a confused hellish state of awareness. But within this storm I had a place to anchor my hope: God would get me through it and had given me a sign in Jesus.

Surprisingly, the idea of going to church or reading a Bible hadn't even entered my mind. Instead, my lifestyle returned to one of drinking, smoking 'puff' and womanising, all to excess, although within all this I couldn't stop talking about Jesus even though I had very little understanding of who he was. I started showing the photos to everyone I met.

I felt like I had a split personality: I desperately wanted to know the reality of this Jesus but couldn't imagine being anything like a religious person. I just thought that somehow God would begin to work in me; all I had to do was fight the evil.

A light was about to shine in the darkness, a voice would call me home, but I would not wish on anyone the way my attention was grabbed.

I was on my way through the old estate to Cockle's house, as my 'puff' / cannabis supply was running short. En route I was walking near to my grandparents' house and I noticed an ambulance parked outside with their front door left wide open. Suddenly I had to make the decision: go over to their house and see what was going on or carry on to Cockle's and score 'puff'. The pull to get the drugs was huge, but I knew that I had to find out what was happening at my grandparents' home.

It turned out that my nan had suffered a massive heart attack. I went inside; she seemed OK and not too distressed, but was being taken to hospital. My grandad was going with her, so I needed to rush straight back home to tell my mother. As I left to return home, I had to push myself not to go via Cockle's house and score. My steps quickened and I eventually broke into a run home. On arrival I broke the news to my mother and we rushed to the hospital in her car.

I constantly thought to myself, *I need to get stoned, I need some 'puff', I need help.* On arrival at the hospital, I had to fight through my own confusion and negotiate with the staff in order to find my nan. Eventually we arrived at her bedside. She seemed relatively relaxed and was more interested in putting us at ease than focussing on her own condition. One of the doctors was trying to communicate some stuff to me, but my mind was all in a haze so I just pretended to understand him. After a while we all agreed that what my nan needed was rest, so we left her and journeyed home. I made the decision not to go out after that but score in the morning instead.

The weekend soon came around and I went to the hospital with my mother to visit my nan. After a few minutes I grew very bored; I felt uncomfortable, mentally unstable and unusually disturbed. After nearly an hour my nan encouraged me to go; she understood how boring it must be for me. As I left, she kept waving to me, as though she knew it would be the last time that I would see her. Later that evening, my mum arrived home distraught and told me and my brother that our nan had died; she had suffered another, this time fatal, heart attack. Mum then began to howl with pure grief.

I was stunned – not with the death of my nan but with my lack of response to it. *Glenn,* I thought to myself, *where are you? Your nan is dead, I know you love her, so why are you not moved?* I began to see how dead I was inside. From somewhere inside I wanted to cry, but there were no tears, no reaction, nothing... I turned to my brother and said, "I need a drink. Coming for a pint?" He looked shocked but came along, probably in support of me.

The days to the funeral went by, with me observing the family grief as though from the outside. They were all torn up with emotion; I just watched, feeling like I was at the theatre watching a dramatic, heartrending story but seated with the actors on stage instead of being with the rest of the audience. All around, the scene played out. I helped with the direction and had a real part in the play, but inside none of it had any base in reality.

Then, one by one, we all filtered into the church hall. The place was packed – family, friends, all had come to pay their respects to my much-loved grandmother.

I looked around the hall, watching the brokenness of many of them: my distraught mother, my tearful brother and my grandfather. How I wished to be a real person, with feelings – alive!

Then the vicar started speaking. His message was a blur: "Yak, yak, yak!"

Give it a rest! I just want to get away, get a drink or a 'puff', I thought as he waffled on.

Suddenly though, it felt as though the speakers were put on full and my attention was grabbed; it seemed that he started speaking to me personally, that somehow through the swell of people all around me, he had focussed his full attention on me and was speaking to me directly. His words echoed through my ears again and again: "You can only come to God as you are! You can't come any other way! He has done it, he has made the way! You can only come as you are!"

My mum, although being profoundly deaf since a child, turned to me and said, "You need to talk to him, don't you?" Somehow had she heard it too, that what the vicar said was for me to hear.

I was disturbed, but there was too much going on for me to talk to the vicar. Even so, the words that he had spoken stuck to me like glue.

Once home from the business of it all, my mother asked me if I wanted to go to church or see a priest or something like that. I knew I had to, so I phoned the local church and made an appointment to see the priest, and my mum offered to drive me there for the meeting. *"You can only come to God as you are. You can come no other way."*

The following Wednesday my mum dropped me off at St Anselm's Roman Catholic Church. Although my family came from a nominal Roman Catholic tradition and most of my schooling had been through Catholic schools, both junior and secondary, I had never bothered with the practice of it; no first communion or confirmation. I had been christened into the Catholic Church, but that decision was made for me and was way before anything I could remember.

Nervously I rang the doorbell to the priest's home attached to the church building. Again my mind filled with darkness: "Kill him, kill him, mess his head up!" voices said through my thoughts.

A middle-aged Irish fellow came to the door and introduced himself as Father Carle. "Come in, come in! Welcome!" he said as he showed me to a small lounge.

I pushed the storm in my mind to one side and tried to engage in normal conversation. Eventually I communicated to him that I was looking for peace with God, that I had been living a very ungodly life but wanted to change, if that were at all possible.

He tried to encourage me and shared a few stories about people whose lives had been dramatically changed through their conversion to Catholicism. We talked for about an hour, and he encouraged me to come to the church service on Sunday night. He also said that it would be good for me to meet with him once a week for an hour or so in order that he could help me with the faith. As I left, he gave me a Bible and said, "Start with the New Testament first; it's easier to read than the Old. Start with John's Gospel." He then took the Bible back and placed a bookmark in it as an aid to help me find where to read from.

I left and walked home feeling very encouraged. I couldn't wait to see what this book had in store for me, plus I now had someone to talk to about the storm that I was living in, someone who had found a safe shore, a lighthouse giving me direction.

When I got home, my mother asked me if I knew who the strange man was in the car park.

"Who? I didn't see anyone in the church car park," I answered her.

"He looked really shifty and he stared at you all the time, watching your every move as you walked around the back of the church," she advised me. "I watched him from the car, and he stayed there sitting on the wall, staring at where you went as I drove away," she continued.

"Haven't a clue!" I answered.

Was I being stalked? Had Cybele got someone from her coven to hunt me down? This just added to the inner confusion that overshadowed me day by day. But I couldn't dwell on the mystery man; I needed to go forward and read the Bible, starting with John.

I had to blink as I opened the Bible. It seemed full of swear words. Then, as I shook my head and tried to see what the pages really held, the swear words dissipated. As I read my way through John's Gospel, another train of thought ran alongside, trying as ever to confuse and fight against me every step of the way. I read and read, working my way through the Bible from that point on. Then came the attendance at my first church service: the 6.30pm Sunday mass.

CHAPTER THIRTEEN

Mass

I joined the throng of people entering the building through the main doors. As everything was unfamiliar to me, I just copied everyone else: dipping my hand in the holy water vessels and making the sign of the cross. Finding a place to stand at the back of the hall, I tried to take part as much as possible. I was sweating and finding it very hard to concentrate.

"Get out of here!" voices raged in my mind.

I did my utmost to take part, but sheer panic and terror gripped my every thought. My mind swooned and the floor became a haze; the wooden floor tiles began to swirl around. My heart was pumping so hard, all I could hear was the *thump, thump, thump* of my pulse. Then it dawned on me: *How can I stand in God's presence?*

I tried as hard as I could to stay calm. I had endured panic attacks since I was a child, fought off all kinds of mind-bending anxieties, but here I felt so exposed and eternally rejected. So often my mind recoiled as I tried to figure out who I was. I couldn't work out my identity, where I began and what I was aiming for; again and again I would just end up in a desperate state of feeling utterly and totally lost. Now, here in this church, amongst all these people, I felt even more lost.

I tried in vain to push through the clouded thoughts and at least pretend that I was becoming good, but instead waves of rejection encircled me. "Unclean, dirty, guilty; God sees you as you truly are!" echoed all around me. "You're not going to make it here, child of hell. Run out! Flee! Get away! GO!" The voices flooded through my mind until I could stand it no longer. Desperate to flee, I looked for the nearest exit then made my departure. I passed through the huge swinging doors and pushed out into the night air.

I wanted to stop and get myself together for a minute, but instead I was engulfed by waves of sheer rejection and fear. Leaning on a wall outside, fearing that I was about to drop dead, sweat pouring down my forehead, I stood and then began to run. *Just run, get away and don't stop.*

I headed down the hill towards the town centre, sprinting, trying to outrun myself. I let instinct drive me on to whatever destination I would reach. Eventually, after more than a two-mile sprint, I found myself leaning on the doors to one of my local pubs, The Plough. Walking through the doors, I managed to order a pint of the usual. How I got the words out, I don't know, but before the beer was placed on the bar, I rushed into the toilet. The next thing I knew, I was leaning over a cubicle, hands fastened on the toilet seat, vomiting as hard as I ever had.

"You okay, Glenn? Where ya been?" an old friend asked, concerned, who had walked in behind me.

After spitting chunks out of my mouth, I answered him, "Church."

"What! Well, that ain't doing you any good, is it?" He laughed awkwardly at my response, believing I was winding him up.

"No, not yet," I answered him while trembling all over.

After consuming a few pints and spirits, my nerves calmed enough for me to set off home.

"I'm sorry, God. I had to run. I couldn't stay. I'm sorry; please help me," I prayed.

I analysed the things that had made me run and found that as I had stood in the church I had become extremely aware of the bad things that I had done and the state of my mind. I so needed to be in that place but found it so hard to stay there. I resolved to press on; all the powers of hell were not going to stop me. Although I was extremely anxious to face that again, I was even more scared not to.

For the next six weeks I tried so hard. I met with Father Carle for our weekly chats, and I told him how hard I was finding it to stay in the service. He would say a prayer for me to keep trying, but each Sunday night the battle intensified.

Every night I was plagued with demonic dreams, nightmares from which I would wake up shouting for help. While awake, blasphemies and murderous thoughts echoed through my thoughts; arguments constantly raged in my mind. I would tell my own thoughts to shut up. I asked God to lobotomise me; I wanted annihilation, peace – but day and night I lived in a haze of confusion. Even my hands would hurt, and my teeth would feel on edge as I felt unseen forces try to force my will to give up and curse God. I truly felt haunted, tormented and near-possessed by malevolent forces. The photos of the door, my Wednesday mornings with the priest and the hope of managing to press on with church were the only glimpses of light in a long, dark tunnel.

A breakthrough came after six weeks of trying to stay in the church service for more than five minutes, to endure the onslaught of the horrors in my head during the 6.30 mass. Finally, I managed to stay long enough to hear God speak to me once again, as I sat in one of the pews, clasping the wooded seat in my hands, literally holding myself down and turning a deaf ear to the constant barrage of vile and blasphemous thoughts that week by week had engulfed me. We were encouraged to stand and sing a couple of hymns, one of them called 'Amazing Grace'. The words to this hymn edified me as I identified every word as my own: "Amazing grace, how sweet the sound that saved a wretch like me. I once was lost but now I'm found, was blind but now I see." *That's my story,* I thought as I identified with every word, but my reality was still that I felt such a wretch and still so lost. Then we sat as the sermon began. Again, I was clasped frozen to my seat, still trying to stay attentive through the barrage of blasphemies. The Bible verse for that week was from Luke 15:11-32 – the parable of the lost son.

"Jesus continued: 'There was a man who had two sons. The younger one said to his father, "Father, give me my share of the estate." So he divided his property between them. Not long after that, the younger son got together all he had, set off for a distant country and there squandered his wealth in wild living. After he had spent everything, there was a severe famine in that whole country, and he began to be in need. So he went and hired himself out to a citizen of that country, who sent him to his fields to feed pigs. He longed to fill his stomach with the pods that the pigs were eating, but no one gave him anything. When he came to his senses, he said, "How many of my father's hired servants have food to spare, and here I am starving to death! I will set out and go back to my father and say to him: Father, I have sinned against heaven and against you. I am no longer worthy to be called your son; make me like one of your hired servants." So he got up and went to his father. But while he was still a long way off, his father saw him and was filled with compassion for him; he ran to his son, threw his arms around him and kissed him. The son said to him, "Father, I have sinned against heaven and against you. I am no longer worthy to be called your son." But the father said to his servants, "Quick! Bring the best robe and put it on him. Put a ring on his finger and sandals on his feet. Bring the fattened calf and kill it. Let's have a feast and celebrate. For this son of mine was dead and is alive again; he was lost and is found." So they began to celebrate. Meanwhile, the older son was in the field. When he came near the house, he heard music and dancing. So he called one of the servants and asked him what was going on. "Your brother has come," he replied, "and your father has killed the fattened calf because he has him back safe and sound." The older brother became angry and refused to go in. So his father went out and pleaded with him. But he answered his father, "Look! All these years I've been slaving for you and never disobeyed your orders. Yet you never gave me even a young goat so I could celebrate with my friends. But when this son of yours who has squandered your property with prostitutes comes home, you kill the fattened calf for him!" "My son," the father said, "you are always with me, and everything I have is yours. But we had to celebrate and be glad, because this brother of yours was dead and is alive again; he was lost and is found.""

As the priest explained the story, I was amazed. Apparently the Scripture readings in each Catholic church are dictated and planned from the Vatican, so each church throughout the world has the same message week by week.

The 'coincidences' in this God-journey were stacking up: the face in the door; the message at my nan's funeral; that song about being lost and found; and the first week that I had managed to stay in the church service there had been a story about a young man wanting to return to his father's house, to receive forgiveness, then the father running to receive his son and then forgiving him and celebrating over him. The priest had said that is what God is like for every sinner who repents.

In my heart of hearts I knew God was telling me that he loved me and had set all this up for me, but I found it so hard to accept. If only I could just believe it. My problem though was that I knew myself too well; I had been myself all my life and always would be, and I knew just how wretched and evil I was and am. *How can God love someone like me?* This argument seemed to pass once again through every synapsis in my brain.

I left the church service encouraged but knew the battle was far from over. I headed down to The Plough regularly, balancing the things of God with the reality of what I was like.

As I entered the public bar, Barry was there to greet me.

"Alright, Glenn? Not gonna puke this week, are you?" he laughed.

"No, managed to stay in the church service. It was good," I answered.

Barry shook his head. "No, not you. You can't be a Christian. This cannot be; it just can't. Not *you!* Anyone else, maybe, but not you, Glenn. I know you; I know the stuff you're into. I bloody know you; you can't be like you one second, then the next a churchgoer. You are about the darkest geezer I've ever known, the devil's own – and now a Christian? Never!" Barry shook his head and muttered. Then, leaving his beer behind, he walked out of the bar and just started to run as he headed off into the darkness of the night.

"What did you do to him?" Malcolm the barman asked me.

"Just told him that I'd been to church," I answered.

"Sarcastic sod!" Malcolm laughed and went off to serve in the Saloon bar.

Soon the public bar crowded out.

"Alright, Mad Dog? Wanna beer?" Morris, an old friend, called over.

The rest of the evening was spent relaxing, playing pool, listening to the music, chatting, drinking and having a laugh.

Barry's reaction wasn't too surprising. He had known me for some time and was aware how I had reacted with venom to anything remotely Christian. But I'd finally done it. I had stayed in church. Now nothing was going to keep me out – *nothing*. I determined that from then on, Sunday evening mass, Wednesday morning with Father Carle and daily Bible reading would become the pattern of my life – but I also knew that I couldn't survive or go on like this much longer in my own strength.

CHAPTER FOURTEEN

Tormented

The torment continued each day and night. The storm clouds of anxiety hung in the air of my mind, threatening to consume me with the unending horrors of complete madness. All I could manage was either to sit alone in my room reading the Bible or sit alone in the Catholic church trying to pray, so at least I was partly functioning. One evening, as once again I sat alone in the church hall appreciating the fact that this building seemed to be always open, I felt drawn to walk cautiously near to the altar. As I neared it, I glanced over to a table with a sign saying "Please Take". There I came across a pile of small pamphlets, and picking one up, began to read it through. The pamphlets were about a St Jude Thaddeus; he was apparently the patron saint for hopeless cases and things despaired of. Immediately I identified myself with him; I felt so strongly that I was a hopeless case, just something despaired of.

I began to conclude that God was directing me here to find these pamphlets. I believed he was guiding me to this patron saint to receive the help that only St Jude could give to hopeless cases such as me. As I read the pamphlet, there were binding promises to St Jude that I was instructed to make and as such he would then intercede for me in heaven before the throne of God. In my confused state I quickly made the promises to give St Jude the glory for the freedom I hoped I was going to find through his intervention. To help me win this battle, I took on a regular discipline of fasting as well as prayer and tried as hard as I could to live in holiness. I began to delve into the histories of many saints, and after reading about the lives of some remarkable saints, I came across the practice of flagellation, where they beat or whipped themselves as an extreme form of penitence. They would punish themselves through these beatings until their spirits broke and they came into full submission to

Christ, thus receiving the freedom they craved in all its fullness. I was convinced that the Lord was calling me to this brokenness; plus, I could also prove to him how much I despised myself and how sorry I truly was. I hated myself, hated life, hated this torment and prepared to beat it all out me. Following the way of penitence, I knelt before a crucifix that hung in my bedroom and made a whip from metal coat hangers. Copying the style of these sincere saints of old, I swished the metal makeshift form of discipline onto my bare back, but the sting wasn't enough so I tried to whip harder and harder. Even when the pain began to take root, it wasn't enough to drive out the torment, so I looked for something more effective.

As I knelt again at the foot of the crucifix, I looked up, ready to start again, but I was unable to continue. Instead, my attention was transfixed on a scene that opened up in front of my eyes – something I can only describe as a vision. I could see Jesus nailed to the cross. In agony of body and soul, he looked down directly at me and called out to me personally, questioning me as I gazed at the horror that he was enduring.

"Glenn, can you add anything to what I have done for you?"

I looked upon him in shame and answered, "No, Lord."

"Then stop trying to and just believe. Just accept that I have done it all for you." These words seem to echo all around me.

I put the self-made whip down, sat on my bed and shook my head, once again realising that I was a total failure and an unworthy recipient of God's reaching out to me. I felt a new, different kind of brokenness inside of me. If self-hatred and penance was not the way to walk, then perhaps self-denial marked the way. I moved my prayers to just asking God to show me his will for my life, for him to guide me and I would try to live a life of submission. But still the peace I thirsted for evaded me; instead of calmness, the battle intensified all the more.

One night my sleep was suddenly disturbed and I felt a presence in my bedroom. Throughout my childhood I had experienced what I can only describe as 'visitations', and I recognised this as another visitation. My bedroom felt charged with an electric atmosphere and I could literally feel the hairs on my arms standing on end. This felt very unlike the LSD flashbacks that I currently suffered from; my head did not have that distinctive 'taste', and the internal confusion of *deja vu* and time displacement were not present. This experience felt very external; the static charge in my room left me feeling very unnerved, and apprehensively I peered around the darkness of the room. Then I saw it and it spoke to me. Its voice wasn't audible but I heard it through my troubled spirit, an inner dialogue. The thing was huge; wider and taller than my six-foot-high wardrobe that it stood in front of. It had the head of a ram and the body of a man. It held up a large sack which had something inside wriggling, as though trying to escape. "In this sack I have your messiah!" the thing boasted to my spirit, taunting me. *Is this a bad dream?* I pinched my arm to check if I was awake; as far as I could tell, I was not only awake but all my senses were telling me this was real.

I had seasons of repeating nightmares and had seen things through my dabbling with the occult as well as experiences of 'visitations' in my early teens and childhood. I had seen weird ghostly sights appear in my bedroom such as a group of people standing over my bed staring at me, a black dog watching me from a table top and even once a donkey that just stood near my bed. These sightings were always transparent and three-dimensional, like a projected hologram. One time I put my hand out to touch an apparition but my hand just went straight through it.

Now again I was alone, sober, looking at something demonic from my worst nightmare, recognising an external atmosphere that to me was a familiar evil, similar to that which I had felt in the spiritualist church. Fear gripped me, but instead of running or trying to hide, an anger arose from the pit of my stomach. I had read in the Bible that Christians have the authority to bind demons and throw them out, so that was exactly what I going to do to this disgusting monstrosity. I jumped out of bed and headed over to it. Then, clenching my right fist, about to jump up and knock the thing right back to the hell it had sprouted from, I shouted out, "In the name of Jesus Christ, I command you to get out!"

Sure enough the thing vanished. Although this wasn't the first time apparitions had appeared to me, it was the first one I'd actually confronted.

This battle was mine, for now, to walk in alone. God clearly had his hand on my life, but to me it still felt like a very fine thread to hold on to. The external visitations were on hold but the internal struggles intensified. I often wondered how I would manage to keep a limited degree of sanity and to continue to function.

I became convinced that many of my problems remained in the realm of the demonic. I had played with fire and got burned, but I believed that Jesus wanted me free. *If I am demon-oppressed then surely I can cast it (or them) out of me,* I concluded.

86

CHAPTER FIFTEEN

The Demon in the Mirror

I read in the Bible that both Jesus and those who believed in him could cast out demons. So one night after suffering a very anxious day through a host of tormenting thoughts, I decided that enough was enough. After I had prayed for a while alone in my bedroom, I walked out to the bathroom, locked myself in and looked at the large mirror fixed on the wall. I was intent to face my enemies. I looked at my mirrored reflection in the eyes, as I had read in the Bible that the eyes are the window to the soul, and said sternly, "If there's anything in there, I command you in the name of Jesus Christ to come out!"

Horror suddenly filled me. The reflection in the mirror was no longer my own; instead, a pale, revolting, evil, expressionless face was looking menacingly back at me. Then an old memory came flooding back. I realised I had seen that face once before when I was about eight years old, at my nan's house. I had looked at the blank screen of her television then jumped back in horror as I had seen this same face reflected back from the corner of the screen.

Instantly my head began to spin out of control; dizziness and darkness engulfed me and I lurched over, having to grab hold of the bath to stop myself falling onto the floor. It was as though I had just kicked a beehive into a small room, and a swarm of angry killers had come upon me.

"Get out of me!" I commanded again and again.

Then my stomach jumped and I vomited. The contents of my stomach looked very odd – somewhat resembling elastic bands. The room seemed to spin around me, and I collapsed on the edge of the bath. Eventually the storm waned and I managed to stand, still very much afraid but with thoughts of protecting my family causing me to act on instinct. The first thing I needed to do was clear up the bath. Unusually, the stench of vomit was absent, so I managed to handle its disposal. Then I scanned the bathroom to make sure it was all clear. As I regained my senses, panic soon engulfed me. *What the hell just happened? I need help.* I quickly exited my house and ran to the Catholic church, heading for Father Carle's house. On arrival I banged franticly on his door until Father Colbert, the head priest, answered.

"Can I see Father Carle?" I asked him.

"No, he's out. Can I help?" Father Colbert replied.

Father Colbert was an older and sterner man than Father Carle; *maybe the right sort of person to help me in this crisis,* I thought.

I quickly blurted out how I was meeting with Father Carle and coming to church, wanting freedom from the occult things I had dabbled with. "I need an exorcism!" I suddenly cried out.

"We don't do those things any more. We don't believe in them here. You played with Satan, now he's playing with you. You trespassed into his territory, now he won't let you go," was his absurd reply.

"I need help!" I answered, looking directly into his eyes.

"Just kick the devil in the head, kick him down and walk in the victory," was his unsympathetic answer.

Kick the devil in the head... I thought about what he had said, and then remembered what the Bible says in James 4:7: "Resist the devil and he will flee." I went calm, thanked Father Colbert for his help, and walked off into the night, hoping once again that I would win this fight. I walked towards the town centre and spent most of the night walking around and around, battling in my head to drive out the constant, destructive, anxious torments of my mind.

As I walked around trying to get some clarity to my thought life, I began to wonder if I was spending too much time alone in my room just reading the Bible over and over. Was I just getting wrapped up in my fears? Did I just need a change of subject? I grew unsure as to whether this lifestyle of a recluse suited me, but the fear was too great within me to do anything else. Perhaps I needed to change the subject, give my brain a chance to rest. Was it possible to just change this whole imprisoning pattern of thoughts and go back to a normal sort of living?

The next day I went out for a walk but only got as far as the corner of my road, a mere fifty metres, before the thoughts came flooding in. *Where can I go to get away from God, to avoid this huge fear of judgement? Where can I hide from God's presence and judgment? If I go to the other side of the world, God will be there. If I go to top of the highest mountain, God will be there. Even at the bottom of the ocean,*

God's there. Even death won't hide me from God. How can I ever find peace? Months later I found King David found peace in the very same thing that then terrified me and he wrote it down in Psalm 139.

One evening I decided to venture back to The Plough, knowing that there was a huge annual party planned. I entered the packed pub and quickly found myself having a few drinks and a laugh with a group of old friends.

I was just unwinding and feeling a bit at peace with myself, when from across the crowded room an old acquaintance came over to me. He was someone I'd looked up to for years, a hard nut from a large, tough family.

"Heard you ain't touched nothing for a few months. Is it true?" he asked, meaning that I was no longer doing drugs.

"Yeah, it's been months since I've even had a draw," I confirmed.

"You?" he answered, looking very confused. "Blimey, mate, you deserve this." He passed me a huge joint that he said he'd rolled especially for me.

"Yeah, I *do* deserve it," I said taking hold of it, remembering the soothing feeling and rush of euphoria I would experience as I smoked 'puff'.

This old friend would often mix a bit of 'smack'[6] in his joints which always added to the experience. But instantly, just as my hand grasped the 'spliff', I was interrupted by a barrage of different and unexpected thoughts. I became extremely aware of what I was about to partake in and the fact that I was giving approval to this destructive way of life. A huge conviction of sin descended on me. "Repent!" flashed through my mind. My heart began to beat very fast, and one by one every eye in the pub turned to look at me. I just stood there, transfixed, the focal point of a drunken mob. Then an internal dialogue with God began.

"Okay, I'll give back the joint, go home and repent then," I said to him.

"Why? Why go home to repent?" was the answer I received.

"Look at all these people staring at me. It's best that I leave now," I explained.

"Why go home? Are you afraid of them?"

---

[6] heroin

"Yes, yes I am! I'll give back the 'spliff' and go home. I'm sorry!"

"Why go home? Whom do you fear, them or me? Whom do you want to please, them or me? Who is important to you, them or me?" God challenged me. My argument was in vain.

With every eye on me in this crowded bar, I passed the joint back.

"Sorry, mate. I can't," I said to my old acquaintance. I then knelt down on the floor, made the sign of the cross and cried out vocally to God asking for his forgiveness.

The reaction from the crowd was instantly very hostile, with jeers and names being shouted at me as I rose from the ground. I pushed my way through the mass of shoulders and headed to the exit.

As I left the pub and listened to the shouts of abuse muffle as the door shut, I soon realised that a chapter of my life had come to an end and the coffin lid put on many an old friendship. I know now that this was exactly where God wanted me to be: alone with him. The words of Luke 12:4-6 were very real to me: "I tell you, my friends, do not be afraid of those who kill the body and after that can do no more. But I will show you whom you should fear: Fear him who, after your body has been killed, has authority to throw you into hell. Yes, I tell you, fear him."

Again it was me, the Bible, Jesus, God, St Jude Thaddeus and once a week Father Carle, but in truth I still felt so alone. Even though I was regularly attending mass, I hadn't got to know anyone else in the packed-out church building. Church seemed to be just a duty for everyone; as soon as the mass was over, they would all leave as quick as they had arrived.

I had lost all my friends except for one: Leon. He would occasionally turn up in his car and insist that we go out for a drink. Most other nights I would sit alone in my room reading the Bible or be alone in the Catholic church praying. Anxiety would often grip me, overwhelming my thoughts. I also sought medical help from my doctor. He suggested that I went to a rehabilitation centre for some specialist help, but I decided not to, just in case the constant barrage of evil thoughts, and my fear that I would one day lose control and kill people, would be exposed and leave me in a straightjacket, locked up somewhere for the rest of my life.

So I just carried on enduring the dullness of thought, the ongoing hallucinations caused by my past LSD usage and the anxiety that pulsated through my body and mind, praying constantly to God, Jesus and St Jude. I would have welcomed any form of peace including death, if only annihilation were an option, but my belief in the afterlife – heaven and hell – were too strong a conviction. Eventually, however, I felt that my life had become a living hell, and this was that point at which I decided to commit suicide, as I described in the prologue to this book.

As you might recall, I heard an audible voice quoting the scripture, "If you pray with iniquity in your heart, your prayers are in vain." I had been fighting so hard to find freedom from my guilt, but this demonic accusation was the straw that broke the camel's back – I lost my feeble grip on hope and felt that I needed to end my life to protect those around me. But then I saw those illuminated words from the Bible on a poster in a school building: "And surely I am with you always, to the very end of the age." Jesus reassured me that he had been with me as my Good Shepherd all along, and finally I found hope flooding into my heart and mind.

With this newfound confidence that Jesus was with me came a growing conviction that there must be a life worth living beyond the solitude I had subjected myself to. Then came the call in a new direction, a road to follow.

I was reading through the Old Testament, when I came across Isaiah 6:8: "Then I heard the voice of the LORD saying, 'Whom shall I send? And who will go for us?' And I said, 'Here am I, send me!'"

I had to stop reading and started to pray all the more. I had heard the call of the Lord and wanted nothing less than to give my life in service to him. I cried out for God to send me to whomever or wherever he wanted me to go.

"I'll go anywhere for you, Lord, *anywhere*. China? India? Africa? Just tell me where and I'll go."

CHAPTER SIXTEEN

In the Bowels of Society

I had heard the call of the Lord, and wanting nothing less than to give my life in service to him, I had cried out for God to send me wherever he wanted. I went to Father Carle and asked him if it was possible for me to become a priest. He could find no reason why not, but as I was still new to the faith, he suggested that I should first seek out regular employment and let God work on my character.

An opportunity came up, and I applied for a job at the local sewerage farm. "Start at the bottom and the only way is up," was the advice given to me. I got the job, but only just; apparently I was the youngest employee ever to be taken on by this local authority for this particular role.

On my first day, after being fitted out with the blue cotton overalls and steel toe safety boots, I was instructed to drive a dumper truck to a location on site known as 'the screens'. When I got there I was met by a group of three workers also in blue cotton overalls. One was operating a mobile crane which had just lowered a large canister into a pit below ground; his name was Trevor. Next to him, communicating with another man down the pit, was a man called Teddy. The man underground in the pit was Stewart.

"Pull up just here," Teddy called over to me, motioning to where I should park the dumper.

Trevor gave me a short rake instrument and instructed, "When the drum comes out we will empty all the grit into the dumper. Rake it flat so that we can keep loading until the dumper is full."

"No problem," I answered.

I looked down the pit and saw Stewart working hard underground shovelling grit into the drum, ready for it to be lifted up by the crane.

"This is the grit channels, the first line of treatment; all the grit that gets washed down the drains ends up here mixed up with everything flushed away, then we shut off the supply and shovel the grit away. It's amazing what we find down here: false teeth, credit cards, money, toys, even bicycles," Trevor explained very proudly.

Then the first barrel of grit was raised up and poured into the bucket of my dumper truck. As instructed, I raked the grit evenly over. I reeled as the stench hit my nostrils, and my stomach turned as I realised the grit was full of turds. The other workers laughed at my reaction. "You'll soon get used to it," Trevor shouted over, "although at first you can't get rid of the smell; it stays with you wherever you go. You'll shower, you'll smell sweet to everyone else, but suddenly as you drink your pint down the pub, that stink will linger in your nose and you'll think everyone can smell it on you." Trevor was the main guy in this little work gang, an old hat, proud to be a sewerage worker and keen to teach all he knew.

Once my dumper was full, I drove off to the designated site to spill the grit. On arrival I stood alone on the marsh banks facing the river Thames and cried out to God, "I can't do this! This is vile; it stinks and makes me feel sick to my stomach. I can't do it!" I stood there hanging my head low; I had a weak stomach for bad smells and toilet stuff; even the smell of vomit made me heave. So I decided to finish the day and never come back.

Then God spoke to my spirit: "I thought you said that you would go *anywhere* for me."

"I meant anywhere in the world," I protested. "India, Africa, China, anywhere you wanted to send me, I would go."

"Then look around you. I am sending you here to be my ambassador to these lost children; tell them about me. Not one of them here knows me. You are my missionary here on this sewerage farm," God stirred in my spirit.

I then realised that his calling starts exactly where we are. If I was to be effective for his kingdom, then reaching the lost starts with the lost around me – but I was not excited about it.

I also began to my see my time in this job as a form of penance. I had lived for myself, and considered that my life and character were probably only fit for this place anyway.

Reluctantly I began my new career as a sewerage plant operative. After my trial period of six months was over, I was called into Stan the foreman's office; he told me that he was very pleased with me, and because of my work ethic they were willing to employ other young people. Sadly, Stan's whole attitude to me was soon to change dramatically, but he was going to become one of God's instruments for working on my character.

I remember the event that caused this pivotal change. Along the marshland adjacent to the sewerage works, piles of white York stones were being stacked, probably for some kind of flood prevention from the Thames. They were very attractive stones and were perfect for garden rockeries. A few of the plant workers were taking them home and I was invited to do the same. I had recently moved into my grandad's home and asked him if he'd like a rockery built in his front garden, which he did, so I took a pile home and built him one.

The next time I met with Father Carle I told him all about it, to which he commented, "So, you are taking home stones that do not belong to you and not paying for them? This sounds like theft to me."

I answered that Stan knew all about it and let us do it, to which Father Carle explained further that if they didn't belong to Stan then it was not his call to let us take them.

I realised that he was right, but as the rockery was built I decided not to take them back and upset my grandad. Instead I would say sorry to God and not take any more.

A few days after I had made this decision, Stan approached me and asked if I would drive one of the dumpers and help another workmate pick up some of the rocks for him to take home. Awkwardly, feeling like a huge hypocrite, I explained my dilemma to him, to which he just shook his head and walked off. From that moment my whole work routine changed.

As usual, the next morning we all gathered in Stan's workshop to receive our daily work instructions. There were fifteen maintenance staff including me under Stan's leadership; he would place us into teams, give us a work chitty and then send us off. This time though, I was held back alone once the other men were gone. Stan gave me my instructions after an introductory talk that went like this: "I am the boss; I give the instructions of what all the men do around here. Have you got that? So if I instruct you to stand on your head and whistle all day, that is exactly what I want you to do, is that clear?" He spoke firmly and directly.

I had a flashback of a situation from a couple of years back in which a workmate from the community programme had spoken to me in a similar fashion. That was the occasion when I had thrown a shovel that near-missed his face. Now, though, I tried to suppress what I actually thought about Stan and just answered, "OK."

He then gave me a list of jobs for me to do which had me running all over the sewerage plant. This was to become his usual practice, and it became a battle of character and wits.

I worked under Stan for over two years before finding other employment. A couple of years after I left, I bumped into Stan's deputy, a man called Ben, who said, "We still talk about you. Did you know that Stan used to make up jobs for you to do in order to try to break you, and you used to drive him mad! He'd work out all sorts of things to get you, but every time he'd give you a duty, you would smile at him, say thanks and walk off whistling. It drove him nuts every time!"

"Oh yes, I knew," I laughed back at Ben. "You see, Jesus told us to bless those who give us a hard time and it puts burning coals upon their heads. I used to walk into his office each day wondering how many buckets of burning coals he wanted!"

Ben laughed and said, "It certainly worked."

One of my duties was the clearing of a compacted conveyer belt in a building that was known as the 'Heaters'. Stan took me over to the top floor of the Heaters building; he then went through detailed instructions regarding how to clear these conveyer belts of the solidified mass of compacted treated human waste that had accumulated beneath the belts over a number of years. I was to be adorned with a hooded green rubber suit and boots, which covered me from head to toe. Armed with a metal chisel, a rake-like scraper/shovel thing which was especially made for the job and a square bucket which was attached to a rope at each end, I began to cut my way through the centre of the compacted poo, making a tunnel which ran centrally under the internal conveyor belt system. Alan stood guard holding the end of the rope and would frantically pull the bucket out to empty it under my instruction. As I tunnelled through the claustrophobic gross mass, I had to keep fighting off panic and sheer revulsion; the stretch of this internal belt system ran for about 40 feet and as well as being surrounded by this brown mass, mechanical noises hummed all around, plus a multitude of worms writhed around me. I was reminded of a scene from the old classic film 'The Great Escape' where Charles Bronson was digging an underground escape route until he become overcome by claustrophobia and panicked. To combat my fears I began to hum the theme tune of this film very loudly. Within seconds the other workers operating their various duties in the Heaters building joined in, including Alan. The whole place was filled with humming and laughter, so after a while I emerged from my tunnel to be greeted by my laughing colleagues and among them a very irritated and red-faced Stan.

The next morning, as per usual, I was held back for special duty. A new job was given to me: cutting and raking acres of grassland, which took about six weeks in all to complete. This meant working alone on a mind-numbingly boring activity. But inspiration hit me: for the grass-cutting I had to wear ear protectors because of the loud noise emitted by the mowers, so underneath them I wore earphones plugged into my Walkman. While cutting the grass I could then listen to Bible sermons for hours, and while raking the grass up I would plan sermons in my head and preach to the trees and wildlife that were all around me. In the midst of the bowels of society I was being fed spiritually by God. I would often get so engrossed by a sermon or particular preacher that I would be late for the set breaktimes at the communal canteen and have to explain to Stan that I was enjoying the work so much I nearly forgot to take a break.

There was a funny order in the canteen, with a set hierarchy of tables and seating orders; the 'popular' employees sat on the best table, of which I had a seat reserved every breaktime.

"Glenn, we got you tea!" my table colleagues would shout every time I turned up late.

Stan sat on the table behind me and would always frown when I walked in.

"Sorry, guys, just engrossed in my work again – you all know I pride myself in a job well done!" I would sarcastically say at the top of my voice.

Although I was popular, there were also some site men who hated me for good reason. Every one of my colleagues knew that I was a follower of Jesus, mainly because I told them all and also was keen to point out that they needed follow him too. I was not always wise about how I went about this. There was one man in particular, Matty.

Matty was the site 'hard nut', a reputation that he deserved. He'd done a few spells in prison for violence-related crimes – a tough, large man with a short temper. I got on fine with him and we had a bit of a laugh, but I had heard that during his last incarceration in jail he'd cracked up because of the confinement. So I had a plan of how to win his soul for Jesus.

One time when we were alone in the pump house, I began to tell him how hell was so much worse than prison, that even in prison there is hope because one day you get out, but hell has no hope. His reaction was not exactly warm to my wanting to see him saved. As I hastily left the pump house, his verbal abuse could be heard echoing across most of the sewerage plant. From that day on, whenever he saw me on site, a barrage of abuse would flow from his mouth, to which I would answer, "God loves you, Matty," and move hurriedly on to whatever duty lay ahead.

A while later Matty did warm to me again due to a particular task given to me once again by Stan. Stan came to me demanding that I stop my raking duty. "I've got an urgent job for you. Follow me." I followed him to the heat exchange system which was external to the pump house where Matty was on duty. This system was used to pump heated human waste in a slurry format into huge tanks, for the production of natural gas, which then powered huge generators, which then powered the plant. Basically, by heating the slurry, the billions of bacteria that bred in it would become very active, and as the bacteria feasted they would 'break wind' causing a huge build-up of methane gas. Apparently, a lot of the fat that we digest passes through us only to congeal again the other side, namely on the sewage treatment farm. This fat can cause lots of problems, one of them being clogging up the heater pipes over time as the slurry gets pumped through them. My new duty was to clear one of these blockages.

The pipes were disconnected at one of the elbow joints and I had drain-clearing poles to screw together and ram down and clear the blockage. Behind the blockage was a build-up of pressure waiting to burst forth, so as I cleared a blockage, a loud noise like a 'wet fart' would be followed by an immediate spurt of hot steaming slurry that, unless I was quick enough to get out of the way, could spurt out all over me. On observing this, Matty eventually came over to me and said, "You know what, mate? We all have our opinions of you being a Jesus freak, but one thing we all agree on, you walk the walk and do what you believe in; we all respect you for that."

A gloating Stan arrived on scene as Matty was chatting to me, but before he could comment I decided to lighten things up a bit.

"Hi, Stan. Have you got any indigestion tablets on you?" I asked.

"Why, do you feel sick?" he answered, still gloating.

"No, I'm fine, but I think the pump house has diarrhoea," I answered, making Matty nearly choke with laughter.

Stan called me to one side and said, "You can worship your bit of wood, but I know what counts: money. It's money that really counts."

At first I thought this was a strange reaction to what was going on, but soon remembered that Jesus said, "As the heart thinks, the mouth speaks."

Another colleague, also called Stan, had a different gripe with me. During a conversation with him I explained that he wasn't a Christian unless he'd actually accepted Jesus as his own personal saviour. The fact he was born in England and had a churchgoing wife was irrelevant. He took huge exception to this and refused to talk to me ever again. This took a lot of discipline on his behalf as, when we were partnered up, I would be as friendly and talkative as I possibly could.

Then there was Tim, a new colleague, slightly younger than me. Tim gave his life to Christ on the sewerage farm, at the screens. He was soon baptised at the local swimming baths, and I began going through the Bible with him. One thing I had to address though, which was once again going to make me unpopular, was the fact that his fiancée was my deputy foreman's daughter and the whole family were involved in spiritism. They had often had private consultation with mediums, so I explained to Tim that this whole practice is satanic, showing him these following verses from an NIV Bible:

"Do not turn to mediums or seek out spiritists, for you will be defiled by them. I am the LORD your God."[7]

"I will set my face against anyone who turns to mediums and spiritists to prostitute themselves by following them, and I will cut them off from their people."[8]

"A man or woman who is a medium or spiritist among you must be put to death. You are to stone them; their blood will be on their own heads."[9]

The fact that I tried to convinced him to end his relationship with her, unless she would turn away from this practice and accept Christ, resulted in a few dramatic showdowns with her family, especially with Ben, the deputy foreman.

Another challenge came from the canteen table. Another new employee, Jim, the cousin of Teddy who shared the popular table, had just started work with us. As we stood in the tea queue, I heard him saying that he didn't know where to sit. The only available table was

---

[7] Leviticus 19:31
[8] Leviticus 20:6
[9] Leviticus 20:27

Stan's, where he sat alone each day surrounded by seven empty chairs. I tapped Jim on the shoulder and invited him to take my chair, while I chose to sit opposite Stan on the lonely table. Stan's face was full of glee when I pulled out the chair opposite him to sit down.

"Been kicked off at last, have you, to make way for your better?" He chuckled at me.

"No, I actually chose to come and keep you company," I answered.

"Yeah, right!" he snorted, refusing to make eye contact with me.

Once the tea break was over, Stan got up to leave, then commented with a smile, "See you lunchtime. I'll reserve you a seat."

A few hours later, when we arrived back at the canteen for lunch, there was a huge kafuffle going on.

"Glenn, Glenn!" the top table called to me as I went to sit with Stan.

I turned to them to see that they had all squeezed up to make extra room for another chair for me so that once again I was being ushered to join them. I turned to Stan, picked up my mug of tea and said, "I'll be off, then."

Then one afternoon while driving one of the dumper trucks, I turned a blind corner and had a head-on collision with a brand-new works van. Fortunately both of us were going less that 5mph so only minor damage occurred and no one was injured. Both Stan and the head office staff had got involved with the incident report, which resulted in a One Way driving route around the blind spot. The next morning Stan called all of the site teams together – every department was there, including the painters, electricians, engineers, as well my usual labourer colleagues – to explain the new driving procedure. Then he went on to state that the whole incident had been caused by me because of my reckless driving, and that a more mature driver would always be observant and have his wits about him. I took a lot jeering from my colleagues, but the next day would bring about a situation that put yet another smile on my face.

Stan was driving one of the brand-new vans on site and pulled over to where I was stationed. He opened the driver's door and immediately a passing dumper truck took it clean off. No one had to say anything; the look on Stan's face as he exited the new, doorless van was worth its weight in pure gold. During our next role call, Teddy couldn't resist saying, "Stan, what was that you said about mature, observant drivers?"

On another occasion, one Christmas Eve, and in keeping with his usual practice, Stan told me to wait behind. After giving me a list of duties, he snapped the following instructions to me: "Do these jobs, then keep out of my way! Today is Christmas Eve, and I don't want to see you. Is that clear?"

"Sure thing, boss!" I replied, giving him a bigger smile than usual.

I rushed around the site completing my tasks with excellence and ease, leaving me with over three hours to keep out of Stan's way. So I made my way over to the screens to get the social club keys from Teddy in order to get in some snooker practice. After about an hour I began to get visits from various colleagues telling me that Stan was looking for me and was getting more and more irate because he couldn't find me anywhere. I just smiled at them all and answered, "Yes, I know. Fancy a game?" From time to time I would peer out of the window and chuckle as I observed Stan's van driving frantically around the site.

Eventually home time came around and, like ants, all the workers made their way towards the changing rooms. As I entered the changing rooms, Stan was waiting by my locker.

"Where have you been? I've been looking everywhere for you!" he bellowed.

"I know you have," I answered with a smile.

"Where have been, then?" he demanded.

"Exactly where you told me to be: keeping out of your way," I answered.

I couldn't believe a man's face could go so purple without exploding. He turned and silently left the building, with sounds of laughter following him from all my colleagues.

"Happy Christmas!" I shouted out to him as he left. Everyone joined in the Christmas cheer.

But shortly after the Christmas holidays, Stan came up with a task that literally had the whole site out watching me. I have to admit, I did antagonise him to set me up for this one. On site were the scraper tanks which held over eleven million gallons of water; both Steve and I were tasked to ride on top of a platform and grease up all the moving parts as well as the miles of cable used to pull the apparatus back and forth. These tanks were so big they could easily hold three full-size football pitches on the base of them. As we were greasing, Steve knocked the grease bucket off the platform – *plop!* – straight into the tank of filthy water.

We set off to inform Stan, but just before we walked into his office, I said to Steve, "When Stan explodes just imagine he's sitting on the loo straining; that will explain his red face."

In we walked and Steve tried to hold back his laughter as I had timed my comment perfectly. Because Steve was unable to talk, I explained to Stan what had happened.

"How on earth did that happen?" he snapped.

I pointed at Steve and said, "It was his fault!"

Steve looked daggers at me as did Stan.

I then went on to explain, "Yep, it was his fault, as I threw the pot at him and he ducked."

Steve turned away as now he was really struggling not to burst out laughing, both because of my statement and Stan's red face.

"No, really, Stan, it was an accident. You see, there are no safety rails or barriers on the platform, so it just slipped in; no one's fault."

The fact that I had highlighted a safety factor made Stan instantly go calm and very reasonable for a time.

After a few days Stan decided to drain the tank, apparently to retrieve the grease bucket. Then after several days of pumping, the tank was empty, revealing huge balls of fat deposited all over the floor of the drained tank, each about the size of a small car. Covering the base of the floor, too, was a half-inch layer of fat, which made manoeuvring around inside the tank very tricky as it was extremely slippery. 'Yours truly' was given the task of breaking down the fat balls and loading the fat into wheelbarrows, which would then be hoisted by crane to the surface for it all to be disposed of.

"What on earth has he got you doing now?" I could hear coming from above, as I watched a crowd gather and lean on the railings overlooking the tank. I was slipping and sliding on all the fat as I wheeled the barrows back and forth. The stench of this fat is indescribable; it takes every effort not to gag. As I struggled on, I glanced up to see Stan in the middle of the crowd, glowing, a huge smile spread across his face; he was chatting away having a great time. Then inspiration stuck me. I had an audience to perform to, so placing my shovel on the barrow, I began to imitate a speed-skater. I was quite an able ice- and roller-skater and found it quite easy to skate on this slippery surface. Soon I was covering the whole distance of the tank at speed, whirling around and around. I then aimed towards the railings where the crowd had gathered and came to an abrupt stop spinning like a ballerina before bowing to a loud applause from everyone.

Stan looked stunned and confused as he saw everyone applauding me. I then looked up at him and shouted, "Hey, Stan. How would you like to come and join me down here? It's great fun! Perhaps we could do a couple's routine!"

But I suddenly felt very sad inside as I saw him turn from the crowd and run away, waving his arms in the air.

Realising that things had become very unhealthy for both Stan and me, I prayerfully and avidly began looking for alternative employment.

God soon opened another door for me, and I found myself literally moving on from the world of overalls and filth to a suited, clean and smart environment. So I drafted a letter of resignation, giving two weeks' notice and handed it to Stan. His reaction was very matter-of-fact, and he even asked me to make sure I was doing the right thing.

Even while I was working out my notice, Stan caused another scene. I was working in the storm tanks with Paul, who was just about the most nervous man I had ever met. He was very jittery, always apologising, and had even fainted because he was once asked to make a written evaluation of a particular job role. Stan arrived at the storm tanks and ripped into the two of us. Paul stood there shaking and apologising, even though we had done nothing wrong, while I simply waited calmly for Stan to stop ranting and to leave us.

Once Stan had departed, I instructed Paul to stay put and explained that I had to go and see someone. I jumped into my dumper truck and tracked Stan down. Stan was at the screens talking to group of workers, so I pulled up near him and called him over. He looked over to me and just waved his arm as if to dismiss me.

"Stan, I suggest you come over here and talk to me, or I'll come over there and say what I'm going to say in front of everyone!" I shouted very demandingly.

He walked over to me, remaining silent.

"You, Stan, are out of order. One: you owe Paul an apology; we all know what he's like and he's done nothing wrong. And two: I don't need a reference from you, so this is how it's going to be while I finish my last two weeks here. You and I both know that you cannot fault my work in my ability, ethic or standard, right?"

"Yes," he answered.

"OK. I'm off in a few days, so I suggest you leave me alone. I guarantee that I will do my best on whatever duty I get, but no more nonsense. Did you know that Jeff the union rep, as well as a few workmates, have told me that I could have you for victimisation? They all know that you have had it in for me. I know it too – I'm not stupid –

but because of my faith I decided to submit to your authority here and work for God. But it ends here. I don't need a reference from you. I will do my job, but get off my back because I've felt like throwing you in one of these tanks – and who knows, it may just happen."

Stan stood there silent for a while and answered, "Fair enough, but did you know that some of my staff asked me not to put you in their teams as they all got sick to death about hearing about this Jesus of yours? No? Well, you made it hard for me to do *my* job, too."

We stood there facing each other for a while, then he turned and headed back to the screens. I drove back to the storm tanks smiling; a huge weight had been lifted from my shoulders.

"You OK?" Paul asked on my return.

"Yes, mate; just told Stan a few home truths. I don't think he'll be bothering us any more. You're doing a good job here, Paul," I answered.

Stan really did do a good job of keeping out of my way and avoiding me for my last few days at the sewerage farm.

Even though I was still there, the battle regarding his authority over me was gone. I felt that it was a good parallel to a Christian life. Even though we are still in the world, we are not part of it, and Satan's power over us is gone; he can only do what we let him, but if we resist him he will flee.

There are enough interesting stories I could tell from my sewage work to fill this whole book and more. But I will now turn to tell how my personal life was developing during this period.

CHAPTER SEVENTEEN

The Path

The job on the sewerage plant had added a few major stresses to my life. I had hoped that filling my days with business would subdue my thought life, but instead I just had to get through each day battling with my messed-up head. I would have to strain to discern what was reality and what was drug damage – or worse – in what would otherwise be normal daily situations. One time when I was in the main office at work, my supervisor Stan appeared to melt in front of me. Although my brain could see this, I recognised that this was not normal and so was just to be ignored. In this way I managed to carry on 'as normal' such that no one else would be aware of the daily battles I was fighting through.

A certain taste would flood through my mind whenever an LSD flashback hallucination was about to take place. After receiving this initial warning, I would prepare myself by picturing an alarm system in my mind, flashing blue lights, sounding off "liar, liar" as the *nee-naw* sound of a security alarm, holding whatever thoughts or hallucinations were trying to swarm through my mind within a secure compartment at the back of my head. Keeping these thoughts pinned down, I could function and face the other battles in front of me, living out a life that appeared near normal to my workmates and colleagues.

Occasionally I would go home heavily fatigued from this mental turmoil, unable to string a thought together. Once when alone at home, I collapsed halfway up the stairs on my way to my bedroom under this barrage of torment; it had left me totally exhausted. Deepest darkness engulfed me once again, and I went physically blind, also unable to speak. I could only think, *bed, sleep, help!* I tried to pray but couldn't remember any prayers, not even the Lord's Prayer, which I had by now prayed hundreds of times by heart. *Saint someone...* (couldn't remember his name). Then, *Jesus, help!* was all I could muster.

Suddenly a new stream of thoughts flowed through my mind: "This is not your battle but God's. Just find your bed and sleep." I groped around on the floor until I found my bedroom and bed, pulled myself into it and lay there trying to remember what sleep was, until finally consciousness fled.

I continued to meet with Father Carle. He was impressed with my changed lifestyle and wanting to be right with God, but often tried to cool my zeal; he would often say, "We can't all be saints now, can we, Glenn?"

Through my reading of the Bible, I also found myself challenging him regarding several church practices and beliefs that didn't seem to fit in with the Bible's teaching. In response he gave me theology books which explained why these practices were so important and not to be questioned.

I pressed on in my desire to become a priest. This world held nothing for me, whilst the Church was everything. To move things on, Father Carle let me take my first communion and confession with him, as I had failed to do these things even though I had grown up in the Catholic system. He also instructed me that I needed to be confirmed before going any further. This confirmation would be a more public event, with the whole congregation present and with a bishop taking the service.

The next confirmation service was planned to take place within a year, so Father Carle put me down as a candidate. I agreed but wanted to know more details as I hadn't come across confirmation in the Bible; I didn't even understand what the relevance of a bishop was.

Father Carle explained, "A bishop is an apostle (the title can be translated either way from the original Greek), and confirmation is your public confession in which you personally acknowledge your baptism and come into the fullness of the Holy Spirit."

"Like at Pentecost! I'm reading through the book of Acts and have just read how people received the Holy Spirit when the apostles laid hands on them," I said excitedly.

"Erm, yes, something like that," Father Carle finished.

I thought, *Wow! An apostle is coming to lay hands on me, and I will receive the Holy Spirit, just like in the Bible!* Sadly, I was very naive.

The countdown was ticking. In just three months' time I would be confirmed a Roman Catholic, and if all went to plan I could be going away to study for the priesthood within a year. With this in mind I could face the trials of the sewerage farm and the battles of life in this world.

With just weeks to go before my confirmation, Leon turned up one Friday night insisting that I would go out for what he described as "a farewell drink" with him.

"OK, but I am not going down our home town and definitely not going in the Bull & Vic pub," I insisted.

After a short walk to his car, Leon realised he had mislaid his car keys, leaving us no option except to visit my old haunts, the local pubs. Eventually we even ended up in the Bull & Vic. I was notorious here: many a drug-related transaction had gone on in this establishment.

Fortunately, although packed out, I could not see any of my old dodgy acquaintances, but I did notice an old friend called Kyle whom I hadn't seen around for a couple of years. I had my photos of 'the door' on me, as was my usual practice, and felt a very strong compulsion to go and talk to him about my newfound faith. Next to Kyle were two attractive blonde girls, clearly with him, one of whom I noticed had been staring at me since I had walked in. With my thoughts fixed on the priesthood, and my repentance of a life filled with womanising, I wasn't looking for female attention. So I turned back to my pint, trying to ignore the compulsion, until I heard a near-audible voice say, "Talk to Kyle and tell him all that I am doing in your life."

Realising that this was God's leading, I headed across the crowded bar towards Kyle. Leon followed me over and within a very short space of time I had engaged him and the two girls with the details of my conversion. They were all genuinely very interested, although one of the girls called Sarah was really irritating me. She was the one who had kept looking at me previously.

She kept asking, "Are you a Christian?" to which I would answer, "Yes, I am a Catholic." "But are you a *Christian?*" she would still enquire.

What is wrong with you? I thought to myself. *I've just explained that I'm a Catholic and shared my experience with you, so what on earth are you on about?*

The other girl was called Diane and was Kyle's girlfriend; she was Sarah's sister.

Kyle and the girls explained that they had recently started going to church as well and that perhaps we could all meet up again. Sarah invited me to come to one of their church services on the Sunday morning. I agreed to, but only if they came to the evening service at the Catholic church.

Next morning I arrived early at the community centre where Sarah said her 10am church service was held. I stood outside watching the people going in. They all seemed normal enough, but no one said anything to me or even made eye contact with me. Then Sarah, Kyle and Diane arrived.

"We wondered if you'd turn up, and we worried that you would be wearing a suit," Sarah said.

"No, take me as you find me; it's jeans and polo shirts for me," I answered.

I joined them and we walked up some stairs to join the service in one of the second floor rooms. This service was very different to anything that I had been used to. There was no priest that I could see; a band played music and everyone sang along. Some people were even dancing; others raised their hands in the air. I thought the whole thing was very weird indeed. Oddly though, while these people sang, I felt what I can only describe as refreshing waves of peace, like a breeze of fresh wind, blow over and through my head. Some of the songs were very nice and the band were pretty good musicians, but I wondered if this was a weird cult, a suspicion that grew as the service went on.

A bloke with a big nose was leading and he welcomed us all to this "Christian fellowship". He then went on to preach from the Bible. I can't remember what he preached about exactly but couldn't find anything wrong with his sermon. I thought that all the men there seemed a bit effeminate; they hugged each other and were all a bit too friendly for my liking. Then, after the service, tea and coffee were served and everyone was invited to stay on, but I had experienced enough and just wanted to get away.

I told Sarah that I had to rush off, and she followed me down the stairs asking if I had enjoyed the service.

"It was *different*," I answered.

She immediately asked if I would come back.

"Probably," I answered.

"See you tonight then. Is it 6.30?" she asked.

"Yes, 6.30 at St Anselm's," I answered her again, thinking at least we would go to a proper church service.

I left Sarah at the door and walked home alone, pondering what I had just experienced. I was very suspicious of the whole group; were they dodgy? The blokes didn't seem that manly. Why didn't these people just go to the Catholic church and do proper church with the rest of us? Perhaps it was my mission to bring Kyle and the girls back to the Catholic Church, I surmised. Perhaps after tonight they would come to realise the importance of the real Church.

The three of them came to the 6.30pm meeting. Kyle, being of Irish descent, was familiar with the order of service, but I could see that both Sarah and Diane were struggling with the whole thing. I took communion alone as they did not go forward to receive the bread wafer from the priest. Then after the service, we headed off to one of the local pubs.

"What do you see in that service? It was really boring!" Sarah said.

"The Roman Catholic Church is the real Church. The Pope can trace his lineage right back to St Peter on whom Jesus built the Church.[10] All the other churches, including your one, are out of sync with God because they have rebelled against his pure Church. Boring or not, it's right!" I answered her, as any good Catholic would.

I had grasped the Roman Catholic theology stance and was now gripped by their doctrines. I believed that St Peter was the first Pope and that from him, right through history until today, hands had been laid from one Pope to the next. I was determined to convince all other believers that they had to come back to Mother Church.

Another line of reasoning that convinced me was that of Jesus placing the centre of his Church amongst the very people that had crucified him – i.e. in Rome – to show his total authority.

But the friendship between Sarah and me deepened, and I spent the next weeks attending both her Christian fellowship and my Roman Catholic church. I grew to enjoy the fellowship service and had checked them out with Father Carle who said they were safe. My mission to

---

[10] Matthew 16:18-19 says, "And I tell you that you are Peter (the rock), and on this rock I will build my church, and the gates of Hades will not overcome it. I will give you the keys of the kingdom of heaven; whatever you bind on earth will be bound in heaven, and whatever you loose on earth will be loosed in heaven."

convince them of their need to come back to Mother Church did not change, and although my suspicions of the fellowship dwindled, a sense of caution about them remained. I would not take communion with the fellowship people in their services as they did not use unleavened bread; I believed that a little bit of yeast could corrupt me spiritually. Moreover, their leader Steve was trying to convince me to be 'baptised' with the Spirit, and I just didn't trust him. Finally, the men hugging each other irritated me, as in my world the nearest one bloke got to another was a handshake.

Despite all this, something in the worship times kept me there; that feeling of the presence of God was all that I really needed. As the band played and the people sang songs to God, I would feel wave after wave of a soothing, intoxicating presence come over me. The feeling was very reminiscent of when I had used heroin and experienced a rush of waves of pleasure engulfing me. It wasn't long before I began to feel guilty about these feelings; after months of repenting over a life of drug inebriation, here I was again enjoying 'a rush'. I decided to talk to a man called Alan, who was Steve's righthand man.

"Hey, Alan, when you lot sing I'm getting heroin rushes," I blurted out to him.

"Pardon?" came his astonished reply.

I tried to explain as best I could to him by repeating myself more slowly: "When you lot sing... I keep getting... heroin rushes..."

"Oh..." There was an awkward pause. "I have no idea what you mean," he responded.

I repeated myself again, this time slowing my words to a near stop, as though trying to explain to someone intellectually challenged.

"When... everyone is worshipping..." I paused to look at his face to see if he was at this point understanding what I was communicating, then continued, "I experience... a wave of pleasurable feelings..." I paused and checked again.

At this point Alan was nodding. I assumed it was because he was with me and not gesturing to someone to come over and distract me until an ambulance and men with white coats would turn up.

"...that reminds me... of when I used to take heroin."

I stopped and watched for body signs that communicated that he had understood the conversation.

"Oh!" he said, this time nodding. It seemed like he now understood what was going on. "That's just you meeting with the Holy Spirit. You know the thing that you cross yourself with in that other church you go to – Father, Son and Holy Spirit? – that's him."

"Who?" I responded, this time taking on the role of the one who seemed intellectually challenged.

"The Holy Spirit. The one that Joel, John the Baptist, Paul and Jesus all spoke about, the one who came at Pentecost. You can read all about him in the book of Acts," Alan replied.

"Oh!" I exclaimed, and then we had a long conversation about what the Bible says about the coming and filling of the Holy Spirit.

I explained to Alan that I had had the same conversation with Father Carle as I was about to get confirmed at the Catholic church. I had asked him what confirmation was all about and he had informed me that it was receiving the fullness of the Holy Spirit.

Over several months I got to know quite a few people in the fellowship and they seemed to like me, even though I argued vehemently with all of them of their need to come back to 'Mother Church'.

Eventually the date for my confirmation arrived. Sarah, Diane and Kyle all came along that dark Wednesday night to the service. I sat nervously at the back of the building, then joined a queue of children, all dressed in their finest, with me at the back in jeans and a patterned blue casual shirt. It felt like no time passed until I found myself there, at this much-anticipated, long-awaited moment of the infilling of the Holy Spirit. I knelt before the bishop, shutting both eyes and focussed on this heavenly blessing, expecting to receive the inner strengthening to overcome all the daily battles that I was enduring. The bishop placed his finger in a thick oil known as chrism, wiped it on my forehead in the shape of a cross, said something about Domestos and it was over.

Nothing, nothing at all happened! There was no infilling, no supernatural experience, no help from heaven. All I got was a sticky forehead.

I stood to my feet feeling totally deflated, not at all exhilarated. *God is not here...* The walk back to my pew seemed to take forever. I was remembering the battles it had taken just to be able to stay in this building, the hope I had found through the story of the prodigal son when I had first managed to stay for the whole service. I glanced around the church; it all seemed so dead and uninviting, and again I thought, *God is not here.* To add salt to the wound, I had chosen Jude as my confirmation name as he was the patron saint to hopeless cases.

Then a new stream of terrifying thoughts filled my mind. I was convinced that I had blasphemed the Holy Spirit and committed the unforgivable sin mentioned by Jesus in Matthew 12:32. In my former life I had blasphemed publicly in every way possible. Cybele had told me about her friends who had blasphemed against the Holy Spirit as they followed Satan. In my arrogance I said that I would copy if she told me what to do; now here I was, battling with a new stream of blasphemies aimed at the Holy Spirit filling my mind.

"You OK?" Sarah asked as I returned to my seat.

"Yeah, fine," I answered in my usual cover-up fashion.

Truth was, though, my hopes had once again been dashed and a new battle had begun. I had expected to meet with the Holy Spirit, to have a new aid in my battles. Instead I just felt heaviness and a deep disillusionment: *God isn't in this place.*

During the days that followed, my thoughts would keep returning to the emptiness of my confirmation experience. I so needed the infilling of God's Spirit. *What is God showing me?*

I still had huge questions about the current practices in the Catholic Church, and the books that Father Carle had given me didn't provide the answers; rather, they tried to convince me that the Pope's infallibility was as important as the Scriptures. This empty experience opened the door to my own personal reformation, as once again God was directing my steps, this time away from the priesthood and even the Roman Catholic Church.

As I dug deeper into the Bible, I found myself agreeing more and more with the Christian fellowship people. I knew I had to make a decision on what path to follow and I saw clearly that many of teachings of the Catholic Church were in direct conflict with what was written in the Bible, but I was too scared to make a final decision. It had been so hard at the beginning of my journey to even stay in the Catholic church building. It was where I had heard God call me his lost son. It was where the devil had battled so hard with me to keep me out. Surely I was called to remain a Catholic? In addition to the spiritual questions, the church building was beautiful, while the fellowship met in a drab hall hired out from the local YMCA. By myself I could not make a decision either way, so eventually God made the decision for me.

I continued to attend both the fellowship and Catholic churches each week, knowing I would have to ultimately let go of one. In my heart the decision to go for the priesthood dominated all my future plans, therefore I figured that the Catholic vocation would eventually win through. Through the fellowship I believed God had shown me another way of viewing Church in order to help me shepherd his people. With this line of thinking steadying my thoughts, I began to get back on track and speak again with Father Carle to press on.

One day I was alone in the middle of a service, enjoying the ceremony of communion. Sarah, Diane and Kyle had stopped coming to the Catholic services, which was fine with me as it gave me head room to just enjoy the religion. I had my head bowed, eyes shut and heart stilled. Then suddenly an audible voice spoke clearly to me.

"Do not worship idols!"

Stunned, I looked up and glanced around to see who had shouted out. To my surprise, the rest of the congregation just remained in a state of silent reflection.

Again I heard, "Do not worship idols!"

This time as I looked around, it felt as though a pair of dark, tinted blinkers were lifted from eyes and I saw clearly around the big hall. Idol worship was going on all around me: people were bowing to statues of Jesus, Mary and the saints, as well as bowing to pictures of the apostles.

Again the voice called, "Do not worship idols! It's time for you to get out of this place – and don't come back!"

Suddenly I felt as though I was being disobedient to God by just being there. I couldn't wait for the service to end so that I could get away.

Is this God who called me into this church now telling me that I have to leave it? I thought the Bible says that God doesn't change his mind? Is this all real, or is this another trick of the devil?

These questions passed through my mind, but whenever I thought about going back to the Catholic church, all I could picture was a sickening vision of idols.

I read the Bible while pondering this major decision about how to move forward with the things of God and found the answer clearly before me in John's Gospel: "He calls his own sheep by name and leads them out. When he has brought out all his own, he goes on ahead of them, and his sheep follow him because they know his voice. But they will never follow a stranger; in fact, they will run away from him because they do not recognise a stranger's voice."[11]

I made an appointment to see Father Carle to let him know my decision to leave the Catholic Church and continue growing in my Christian faith within a Free Church setting. He was upset but supported me in my choice, as he acknowledged that I was still trying to follow Jesus and trying to be obedient to him. My Catholic chapter had come to an end.

---

[11] John 10:3-5

CHAPTER EIGHTEEN

Chains are Broken

So much can happen in a short space of time, and this was exceptionally true during my early time at the Christian fellowship. Once I had made my spiritual home in the Free Church, my faith was one shared with likeminded believers. There were prayer meetings in the mornings, evenings and even on the weekend nights. Even though the usual battle raged on in my mind, I continued somehow to keep going forward.

Sarah invited me to go to her brother Paul's house for a Sunday night prayer meeting. It was an exciting place to be. Paul was a very zealous young man; he too was quite a character – an ex-hooligan with a large reputation. His house was full of people in their twenties crying out to God for breakthrough for revival. As I left my house with Sarah to make our way to Paul's, I once again began to experience what I perceived to be an LSD flashback.

I noticed that every small detail on the brush side of the leather on my deck shoes fluttered and swayed, like a field of grass being blown in the wind. Trying to ignore what was going on, I engaged Sarah in conversation as we walked to Paul's, but by the time we arrived my head felt like it was about to explode into a full-blown anxiety attack. I could picture monstrous faces contorting and tormenting my thoughts. "Blaspheme, kill them all!" voices in my mind said over and over again. I just sat silent, holding myself together as the others prayed out loud to God.

Suddenly a girl called Helen screamed. "I can see hideous, demonic faces all around us."

The atmosphere in the room changed as a few more screamed out, "So can I. I can feel evil all around us!"

I knew this was emanating from me. What they could see were the very thoughts I was trying so hard to contain.

"I'm sorry," I said jumping to my feet. "It's coming out of my mind; it's all coming from me."

I shot out of the meeting and into the night, remembering times that I had practised thought-projection, an occult practice that enabled me to put thoughts into others' minds. A feeling that was very familiar to me engulfed my entire being once again. I had suffered episodes like this ever since being a young child, where my vision somehow seemed different, I had feelings of *deja vu* and an impending sense of doom dominated me. I could remember times when I had had such episodes and my nan would walk me around the estate streets at night, telling me to pull myself together or I would end up in the madhouse.

"Wait!" Paul shouted to me before I could disappear. "You don't have to suffer alone. I'll take you to our pastor Steve's house; come with me!"

As we paced our way up the hill towards Steve's home, I explained to Paul that what they had seen was the state my mind was permanently in. "Even now I have voices telling me to kill you," I said.

Quickening the pace we eventually arrived at Steve's house. Paul and Steve had a chat, then Steve invited me to sit in his study.

"You need to be baptised in the Holy Spirit. God's indwelling presence will help you in all your battles," he explained.

"OK then, please pray for me. I don't know how long I can go on like this anyway," I answered – still reluctantly but now surrendered.

They both placed their hands on my head and prayed.

"Did you feel anything?" they asked after a while.

"No, nothing," I answered honestly.

After a long discussion and more prayer, Steve suggested we pray again at church the next Sunday, and Paul and I left to go to our own homes.

On top of all my present anxieties, I now had this new fear of a disrupting evil presence that could spill from me and frighten my would-be friends. Perhaps I was unsavable after all; perhaps I had blasphemed the Holy Spirit and was truly lost; perhaps all these battles were just death pangs for me. I had no option except to continue my endurance.

At the fellowship, the leaders had gathered with me to pray regularly. They prayed repeatedly for me to receive the Holy Spirit, and also for me to come into more freedom, but in reality nothing seemed to change.

Then a sign of breakthrough came.

Steve's wife Alice said that she received a 'picture' from God – an image placed into her mind that related to my circumstances. She said she could see a tightly closed rose bud, and a wall encompassing or protecting someone, then an egg with a very hard shell. She said I was the rose that had to emerge, but that I had built a wall of defence all around myself; now it was time to bring down that wall.

"How?" was my simple response, but she did not really know so she said, "Just trust God."

During the next Sunday worship time at church, a man who was standing to my right began to wail and cry intently. He was a visitor to the church, and I began to grow very irritated by his sobbing. I thought to myself, *I wish this bloke would just shut up.* Then he blurted out between sobs, "These tears are not my own. They belong to someone else who has just shut down inside."

Bang! It hit me full on. Something popped inside me as he said this. Suddenly I was overwhelmed with grief and began to cry. *No!* I protested to myself. *God, I couldn't even cry at my own nan's funeral; I haven't been able to cry for years. I'd forgotten how to feel, so why now in front of all these people? This is so embarrassing!*

"I care more about you than your feelings of embarrassment." Again I recognised the same calming voice of Jesus speaking to me, leading me closer to him.

Once again I found myself running out of a meeting, and once again someone intervened. This time Alan had followed me out, and he asked what was going on. I explained how I had been unable to feel any emotions for years and now this 'visitor bloke' had done something to me. He took me into an empty room and offered to pray for me. There he invited the Holy Spirit to come and took authority over anything demonic. As he prayed, the door to the room suddenly slammed shut by itself, leaving us shut up all alone in this empty hall.

"Now, that was weird…" Alan said a little bit shaken, after which he quickly said amen and led me out to the hallway. He then reassured me that all the leaders were meeting regularly to pray for me and my problems. Eventually, though, they all admitted that they had turned me over to God, as humanly they ran out of ideas of what to do to help me.

A few weeks later Steve and Alice invited me and Sarah to go to a meeting which was led by a visiting team from the Vineyard group of churches. We were told that "at these meetings all heaven breaks loose" and people were being healed and set free as the Holy Spirit fell in power.

The meeting was on a Wednesday evening, and we arrived at 7pm to an already crowded meeting that was not intended to start for at least another hour. As the people stirred and milled around, I experienced an intense anxiety attack and asked Steve to pray with me, which he did immediately.

The worship started and I could only just about hold myself together. Then I felt a refreshing breeze sweep over my hot, confused head. I looked around to see if there was an open window or fan or air conditioning system nearby causing the breeze. I could see none, but this breeze felt so refreshing and brought real peace to my mind. After the worship and a bit of Bible teaching on the coming kingdom of God, we went into a short breaktime, during which an offer for prayer was given by the Vineyard team. I went and spoke to one of the team members about all I was going through.

"Come and see me after the service. We like to deal with the difficult ones at the end," was his reply to me.

Although in hindsight his words could have sounded a bit off-putting, the way in which he spoke them, the spirit behind his words, strangely put me at ease.

The service flew by, and at the end there were many people being prayed for by the team. I saw the man I had spoken to looking around the room until he met my eyes, then he motioned me to come over to him.

"Wait here; we will all be with you in just a moment," he explained.

Steve came over and waited with me, then four of the team came over to us and the lead man asked who Steve was. He listened to Steve for a while and then said that it would be best if he waited for me outside the room in which they were going to pray for me. Steve looked indignant as he wanted to be part of the prayer process that this team were going to take me through. The lead man, though, graciously but firmly reiterated his request that Steve would wait.

Then they invited me into a small room and asked me to take a seat. The prayer team consisted of three men and one woman. The lead man was a huge black man, whose name turned out to be Stu; he explained that back home in USA he was a policeman as well as part of the Vineyard leadership. He sat opposite me and asked me to look at him.

As I tried to do so, I began to grow very angry and agitated, even growling under my breath.

"Look at my face and into my eyes, as the Bible says the eyes are the window to the soul," he said.

As I glanced into his eyes, I turned away in a flash, unable to hold a focussed stare. Feelings of shame, guilt and uncleanness emanated all around me. *I daren't let him see inside my soul.* Then the battle in my mind flooded to the forefront: "If you let him pray he will cast you out into hell. You're the demon, can't you see it? You will be lost if you let him in." I grabbed the chair arms as I felt myself losing grip from within.

"Look at me!" Stu demanded.

"I can't. You don't understand," I answered, feeling I would be lost forever.

"Look at me!" he demanded again.

Grasping the chair arms intently and keeping my gaze to the floor, I growled back, "No!"

"In the name of Jesus Christ, I command you to look at me!" he said sternly.

Immediately I lost control and my gaze was drawn to stare intensely into his. We sat there looking each other full on, eye to eye.

"Is this you, Glenn, or am I talking to someone else?" he asked.

"It's me and I'm scared," I answered.

"It's OK. We are here with you. Come, Holy Spirit!" he said, this time gently.

Suddenly my head was flung back. It felt so heavy I could not support it, and it hung backwards over the neck of the chair. My arms and legs began to shake involuntarily, the right side of my face went totally numb, then my whole body began shaking from my feet to my head as my grasp of the chair arms went tighter and tighter. I felt as if I were in the middle of a storm. There seemed to be huge dark clouds gathering all around me, intent on my destruction, and yet at the same time there was a small voice close beside me speaking calmness to my soul.

Through broken speech I asked for someone to support my head; I was actually chocking from being unable to lift it and bring it forward. Stu carried on praying for me as the others began to ask questions. It was as though they had all gained access to my most personal life diary (if I had actually kept one); they brought up sin after sin, experience after experience. Each time, they asked me to repent and ask forgiveness of what they had identified from my past.

"If the Son sets you free, you are free indeed. In the name of Jesus, be free!" Stu commanded.

I shook again from head to toe, then slumped in the chair, this time to be engulfed with what felt like liquid peace. I began to feel intoxicated, as though I had just binged on fourteen pints of strong beer.

Eventually I staggered to my feet and was greeted by hugs from the team.

"You will have to walk in your deliverance. Keep walking the walk of faith. Jesus loves you, he died for you, he has chosen you and will not let you go," Stu told me before passing me over to the waiting Steve.

Steve drove me home, which was very fortunate as I did feel very drunk.

———————————

I had a doctor's appointment a few days after, as my family doctor was still insistent that I should go to a drug rehabilitation centre to help me with my recovery. As I walked into his office he immediately remarked, "You're better! You just look so much better! What's happened?" I explained to him about the prayer ministry that I had just received, to which he answered, "I don't believe in that sort of thing, but I can see by your countenance, just by your appearance, that something dramatic has happened to you." After an initial check-up, I walked out of his office smiling, leaving him looking bewildered.

I believed I was on my way to freedom, I felt more empowered, but had to battle to keep my mind set straight and walk in this freedom. I had been prayed for to receive the Holy Spirit, I had met with the Holy Spirit, I had felt the presence of the Holy Spirit, but was I actually *filled* with the Holy Spirit and using his gifts?

The following Sunday at church, Steve asked me to share what God had done for me at the Vineyard meeting. I stood and recalled everything that I could remember. I was surprised at how many came up to me and said that my story had really blessed them, but what surprised me most was that I assumed they would hear about this kind of stuff all the time, seeing that they claimed to be a church that instead of being a traditional church were biblical and 'New Testament' in their style.

After the service, Steve and Alan asked me if I would like them to pray for me to receive the gifts of the Holy Spirit mentioned in 1 Corinthians 12 and 14. I was familiar with these verses and had also read that we should eagerly desire them and that they must be used for the strengthening of the church, but I had assumed that they were for special people, maybe just the leaders. Steve explained from both the Old and New Testaments how the gifts were promised for all believers and that they were not an optional extra.

Eagerly, I asked them to pray for me.

"OK. What gift do you want, then? Tongues, prophecy or what?" was Steve's pragmatic response.

"Oh, all of them. I want them all," I replied.

"It's usual to just get one," said Alan. "How about the gift of tongues?" he continued.

"OK, that as well. *I want them all.* If we are to eagerly desire them, then I want all of them," I enthused.

"OK then, we will ask God to give whatever gifts he wants to give you, but we will ask him to give you the gift of tongues as confirmation that you have the Holy Spirit," Steve suggested diplomatically.

The leaders laid their hands on me and prayed. Then after a while, they asked me if I had felt anything special, or if God was saying anything.

"Not really," I answered.

So they prayed a bit more and then told me to claim by faith that God gives the Holy Spirit to all who ask and to try to talk in tongues.

Not much happened for at least the following two weeks. I was increasingly walking in my newfound freedom, but my head was still very cloudy and confused. I wanted more breakthrough and especially to see the biblical and right supernatural presence manifest in my once-dark life.

I was in the habit of fasting for breakthroughs and decided to fast for a few days from food to receive the gift of tongues and prophecy. After the fast, still nothing happened, until I was given a special job to do at the sewerage plant. Stan had sent me over to another site on the marshes to clear all the grounds around the unmanned pump station. I loved this task as I was completely left alone, cutting grass with the industrial mowers and able to pray out loud with real freedom. It was a hot, sunny afternoon and I was cutting some long grass that had grown up along the steep banks that led up to a very large holding tank. I was getting very irritated by a swarm of flies that enjoyed hovering above the petrol engine of the mower, so from time to time I would swish them away with my T-shirt that I had removed because of the heat. Then, from out of nowhere, a huge oppressive feeling surrounded me, that familiar acid taste filled my mind, the grass around me began to swirl causing familiar patterns to emerge that I had observed during many an LSD trip, and as I looked up I could see a huge flying saucer hovering above me, as clear and as real-looking as the mower I was holding on to.

"This is stupid!" I shouted out. "I don't even believe in UFOs!"

Then from the depths my soul I began shouting in another language, sentences flowed from my mouth. Oddly, I was in complete control of what I was saying but didn't have a clue about what the words meant, although one word that I repeated again and again was '*shammah*'. As I shouted out in this 'language', the hallucination dissipated and the 'acid' taste ebbed away, both being replaced by feelings of peace and wholeness. I had found myself speaking a strange new language and it had brought about a new level of breakthrough: the end of the plague of hallucinations and LSD flashbacks. I received my healing.

If only I had not been such a sceptic and more doubtful than the disciple Thomas! Yet God loves the sceptic and the doubter, and he was ready for my wandering ways. You see, after a few days I began to think the whole situation had just been my imagination running wild. I even felt too embarrassed to pray in this new 'language', as it just felt like I was making it up, talking gobbledygook like toddlers do when they play.

One day I was studying the Bible alone, as was still my habit, and I was using a Bible handbook which explained in depth the history around passages, giving detailed backgrounds and translations from the original Greek or Hebrew languages. Then I saw a word that I had begun to use more than any other in this gobbledygook language; it was there in this handbook, a Hebrew word literally meaning 'The Lord is there' – '*shammah*'.

There have been, and continue to be, so many coincidences in my life of the reality of God that I wonder why so often I doubt – but I have come to accept that God is gracious towards me and has a full understanding of the battle in which we stand here on the earth. His name is '*Jehovah Shammah*' – 'God is there'.

CHAPTER NINETEEN

A Road Not Easily Walked

In a previous chapter I touched on how Sarah and I met. God had clearly orchestrated the whole evening, but what I didn't know at the time was just how much detail and planning God had put into it!

That evening Diane and Kyle had been trying to convince Sarah to go out with them, but she had been reluctant to go as she didn't have a boyfriend and didn't want to 'play gooseberry' as the saying goes. Sarah, being unimpressed with the young, free and single males at her church, didn't have any hope of meeting one any time soon. Diane suggested Sarah should pray and ask God for a Christian boyfriend. In her naivety she worried and wondered if she could ask for that. They decided it should be OK as the Bible says we can ask God for anything. So she said a simple prayer there and then, and decided to head out with them after all.

On walking into the Bull & Vic pub, Sarah saw me from behind, standing at the crowded bar, and heard in her head, "You're going to marry that man." Thinking she must be going a bit crazy as she'd never met or even spoken to me, she kept the thought to herself, all the while wondering why she had thought it.

I was feeling very confused by being in this particular bar after having sworn I would not set foot in there. But while standing at the bar, I looked around and noticed a stunning blonde looking at me; she looked away shyly each time she noticed me returning the glances.

Now, you must realise I was preparing for the priesthood and a life of being a celibate single man, but I admit I enjoyed this beautiful blonde looking my way; what a dilemma she caused me!

I walked over with the intention of talking to Kyle; he was an old acquaintance I had not seen in years. I relished the opportunity to tell him what God was doing in my life and show him my photos of the face of Jesus. Sarah spotted the cross I was wearing round my neck and went on to interrogate me, wondering why I, a tattooed 'man of the world' was wearing it; was it a fashion statement or something meaningful? She kept asking if I was a proper Christian. It was very annoying as I'd already told her I was Catholic. After chatting a while and showing my photos, we agreed to meet again at each other's churches.

It was July when we met. By September we had decided to marry, making it official with our engagement in October. Our wedding was the following June, just eleven months after we met. All the usual expected securities for starting out married life together were simply not there for us. We just knew our life together would be an adventure, so with no savings (in fact, no money at all), no great job and no home of our own, we forged ahead and tied the knot. It caused a few raised eyebrows when Sarah told her pastors she had prayed for a Christian boyfriend, met him down the pub, and he was a reformed drug-using criminal who was planning to be a Catholic priest but was now giving that up so they could get married.

Our story may not be considered a recommended route to finding a spouse, but in my defence, on writing this we have just celebrated 36 years of marriage. Together we've gone through many adventures, hardships and heartaches, but with much laughter and love all the way.

An opportunity arose before the big day for us to buy the council house I was sharing with my old grandad at a huge discount, but after praying we were both convinced it wasn't the right thing to do. We independently felt God tell us to wait and see what he could do instead. So we made the decision to "seek first the kingdom of God and his righteousness", trusting, as the Bible says, that he would give to us the things we need. This meant that when we returned from our honeymoon, we would have no place of our own but simply stay here and there with family and friends, hoping that something would eventually work out.

After four months of being married, Sarah became pregnant and we were expecting our first child. This was the point at which I changed jobs and moved from the sewerage farm to an office environment with a local paper in the hope of earning more money. Then, halfway through the pregnancy, while I was away at a church leadership conference, a complication set in. I arrived home late on a Friday evening. Sarah was six months pregnant and she was staying with her family. She said that during my week away the baby had hardly moved, and that she felt very unwell, dizzy, and had fainted earlier in the week.

Back then there were no weekend or out-of-hours midwife units, so Casualty was where we sought reassurance. We were ushered into a room for a monitor to be strapped on to check the baby's heartbeat.

Nothing. No reassuring beat.

A friendly nurse said, "Don't worry; let's move the monitor."

Still nothing.

The monitor was changed. "It must be faulty," we were told.

Still nothing.

More staff came into the room, but now the smiles were gone from faces after an hour of trying. Now there were just looks of serious concern. Understanding what terrible news we were facing, I began praying continually under my breath.

The doctor came and said, "I'm so sorry. This is so difficult to hear but it looks as though the baby has unexplainably died."

I continued praying and refused to accept the news. I asked them again to try to listen for a heartbeat. Using a small handheld device they tried again, and we heard a slow *whoosh*. Just for a moment our spirits lifted.

"That's *Sarah's* pulse you can hear," they told us.

Through tears and numbness a plan was made for us to go home and to head back in if and when signs of labour started, with an appointment given for first thing Monday to be admitted if not already in hospital. With a surreal sense of the world closing in, we tried to make sense of what was happening, whilst praying and hoping against the odds our baby could still be alive.

It took all our resolve and strength to go to church Sunday morning when what we wanted to do was to hide away at home on our own. Reminding each other we would always "seek first the kingdom of God" we headed to church. Sarah insisted, however, that I was not to talk to anyone about what was happening as she simply couldn't cope with the attention we would undoubtedly receive. We planned to slip away quietly at the end.

During the worship time a man stood up and said God had told him that there was someone at the meeting having a difficult time with their pregnancy. Knowing there were many couples expecting at the time, we looked around but just knew this 'word of knowledge' was for us. We agreed to let him pray for us, without giving him any information about our situation. As he prayed, Sarah felt a surge of pain through her stomach and a jolt as the baby moved.

Whatever happened when he prayed, even to this day we don't know for sure, but on arriving at hospital early Monday morning the first image an ultrasound monitor showed us was a tiny hand giving us a thumbs up sign and a little heart beating. Amy was delivered, a healthy but tiny baby, a few weeks later.

By the time Amy was born, we were living independently in an expensive studio flat, and then came a journey of bouncing around from home to home. After the flat we lived in a four-bedroom detached house for a lower rent, and then we were made homeless as the house needed to be sold just as Sarah was ready to give birth to our second child, Alice. We had given our word that as soon as the owners of the large house needed it, we would move on. The problem was that we just couldn't find anywhere that we could afford.

The council warned us that if we just moved out we would be 'voluntarily homeless'. However, after going through a very awkward process, we were given temporary accommodation by the council. It was a real 'dump', and our second child was due in less than three weeks when we moved into this shared house. It looked derelict, with bare floorboards throughout and a family living in two rooms downstairs. We were shown upstairs and walked into a room that was supposed to be our living room and kitchen; we reeled as it stank worse than a public toilet. Every room had a Yale lock on it and we were given two keys; one to this stinky room, the other to our bedroom.

Fortunately a group from the church came over to help clean the rooms.

"You can't move in there," one of the pastoral team said.

"We have no choice. Where else can we go?" I answered.

The team scraped stuff off the floor, bleached everything everywhere, and scrubbed and cleaned throughout, so at least it was a clean hovel.

We were in there for just over a week when a council official came around and told us that we now had to move to the rooms downstairs as the other family were moving out and a new person was moving into our upstairs rooms. We all had to share the bathroom and toilet, but at least the move downstairs gave us a separate private kitchen, so at first we thought it a positive inconvenience – until we ventured into the rooms. A familiar stink hit us again; the family that had resided there were responsible for the filth. There were urine-soaked floors; polecats had been kept in the kitchen; and a mound of filthy nappies, dead polecats and other rubbish had just been thrown onto a huge heap in the back garden. As Sarah was days away now from giving birth, I sent her out as I attacked this cesspit of a home. Eyes streaming and retching constantly, I swept up piles of maggots ready to turn into flies, scrapped gunk off the floors, and bleached and disinfected the whole of the downstairs rooms. Then I phoned the council to get rid of the huge pile of filth in the garden. I explained our circumstances but they denied liability. So I just dowsed the pile which was around ten feet high with petrol and any combustible fluid that I could find and set fire to the lot. We then stayed at Sarah's mum's house for the night.

The following morning, feeling weary, I said to Sarah, "All we need now is for Hell's Angels to move in upstairs."

My prophetic gifting was sharper than I thought. The next day we got back to the house and, as we walked in, I heard God whisper in my ear, "Change all the locks." To Sarah's bemusement I busied myself swapping all the lock barrels from the doors upstairs with the ones downstairs.

Shortly after completing the task, a woman came into the house and, before even saying hello, walked up to our bedroom, pointed to it and said, "That room is my storeroom."

"No, that's our bedroom. Your rooms are upstairs, and we share the bathroom and toilet," I explained to her.

"It's my storeroom and I have the key to prove it!" she demanded indignantly.

"Really? Try your key, then," I challenged her.

She tried a key that somehow she had managed to get that should have fitted that lock, but it would not turn.

I smiled at her and said, "If you try that key in one of the upstairs locks, I am sure you will find it fits."

She stormed off, only to return later with a whole chapter of Hell's Angels. (Sometimes, when you think some things just can't get any worse, believe me, they can.)

Just before the move, we had been asked to host a 'home group' so decided to carry it on in this place, but sadly our members felt very intimidated when they came over and found the house full of drug-taking, motorbike-riding, unwelcoming satanists.

Alice was born, and to add to the problems we had experienced, a nest of bees had decided to make home in the cavity of one of the internal walls and were swarming throughout the house as we returned from the hospital. Once again, when we contacted the council they denied any form of responsibility. So, armed with an insecticide powder, I found the nest and wiped them out.

Unfortunately I could not do the same with our other house guests, and things were very tough, especially with a young daughter and our baby Alice. Work too had its demands, as well as the pressures of church leadership. We had somewhere to live, but it was not under any circumstances a home. This chapter of Hell's Angels practised a lot of satanic stuff in the house, and I would leave Bible tracts and passages all around the place. The woman also had a young daughter who managed to pass on a very nasty chest infection to our baby Alice.

We could see no relief to our housing problems, and one morning during my habitual prayers, I cried out to God, "You told us not to purchase my grandad's house, even though it was so cheap. You said to trust you and see what you could do! Is this it? Is this the best you can do? I am not impressed!"

Suddenly everything in the room went very still, including me, as I heard an audible voice say, "You will have a big house soon."

That was it. That's all this voice said, but strangely that was all that was needed.

I walked into the bedroom and said to Sarah, "God's just told me that we are going to have a big house soon."

She laughed and said, "How's that going to happen?"

"He didn't tell me that bit, but I know it will happen," I answered.

Sure enough, within two weeks we were given another 'temporary housing' – a huge detached house on its own grounds. It was a real dream home and a place of recuperation. We danced around together in the gardens and could not believe that our God had truly brought us into a place of blessing.

After a fair while I knew that I could live in that house for the rest of my life; I truly loved it. I even heard God give me the exact figure of what I could purchase the property for. The market value, then in the 1980s, was £250,000; the figure God gave me was £70,000. Today the house would be worth in excess of a million.

We lived in that house for a great couple of years. I also found a new job working for a local newspaper, which I will cover in more detail in the next chapter, and we felt truly blessed. One morning I was driving down our long drive in my brand new company car, listening to worship tapes. When I came to the end of the drive, ready to turn onto the road, I noticed a very familiar face standing in the front garden of a small bungalow opposite. I opened my window, flashed my lights and tooted my horn to attract his attention. He looked over, saw me and tried desperately to ignore me.

I drove out and stopped just near him, leant out of the window and called, "Good morning, Stan, my old supervisor from the sewerage farm! I didn't know you lived here. I'm your new neighbour. I live in this house at the end of the drive."

He stood there open-mouthed as I drove off in my new car, wearing a new suit and living in a dreamhouse. I wonder if he pondered those words he had once said to me: "You can worship your bit of wood; its money that counts!"

I still look back on those 'South Acres' days (the name of the house) as a time of extravagant blessing. Then one morning, just as we returned from a church camp, there posted through our letterbox was a key to a permanent council house ready for us to move into. Confusion rang in my ears; the head of the housing department had told me that we could stay in South Acres indefinitely, as if they changed tenant the rent would at least triple. I had heard God say that we could purchase it; he had given me the figure. The house they wanted us to move into was on the same road where my grandad lived; I'd be paying more in rent than I would have done with a mortgage. It was also just five doors away from the house I had grown up in and opposite another house where I had previously dealt drugs from – right back in my old haunts, but now with my precious family. Surely this could not be God!

I spoke to the head of housing and asked him what was going on. He said, "It's your decision. You have a contract to stay where you are, but we have a problem housing a family with four children; we can't find any suitable properties for them and it looks like we will have to split them up in order to house them."

Straight away I thought of what Jesus said in Luke 6:30: "Give to everyone who asks you, and if anyone takes what belongs to you, do not demand it back." *No this can't be right. Surely Satan is trying to steal my blessing.*

Pastor Steve and I had become very good friends, and he had also become my mentor. I ran most of my major problems and decisions through him to get his wisdom and insight, so at our next meeting I spoke with him about this housing issue. He came over to South Acres, looked around and questioned me saying, "What are your motives for staying here?"

You got me! I thought inside, as I could hear God speaking through this huge question. What *were* my motives to stay? I could think of only one: to be blessed!

Steve left and God kept pushing the button. Then he spoke: "You can stay here with my blessing, you can stay here and be blessed, or you can be where the people are."

I knew how I should respond, but I hated the idea. I knew that God's calling on our lives was to be where the people were. How could I justify hiding away, living a life of just being blessed?

I informed Keith, the head of the council, and he set up a meeting with me. As I walked into the council offices, one of his staff came over to me and shook my hand.

"We all know that we owe you a big thank you!" he said.

Keith too was very appreciative; he was also a Christian and offered to support our move in prayer.

Then I went to view our new house.

CHAPTER TWENTY

A Taste of Revival

King David, the man after God's own heart, once said, "I will not sacrifice to the LORD my God anything that cost me nothing."[12] When I was first saved I had asked God to allow me the privilege of giving him things that cost me, so here I was, kneeling on the bare floorboards in a house back in Willow Road, the road that I had lived in during my days of rebellion. I wept as I looked back at the blessing of South Acres, trying to accept the fact that I was back here ready to bring up my family where I knew that drugs, violence, immorality, hatred and witchcraft were the norm.

As I knelt there, unsure of how we were going to cope, I once again heard that assuring still, small voice: "I will protect you, just as I did Daniel when he was plunged into the lion's den. I will shut the mouths of the lions and you will be at peace here."

"Thank you, God. I need you more today than I have ever done," I answered.

The day we moved in was awful. Our furniture just did not fit in the two-up, two-down small terraced house, so we just had to leave it in the garden and sell it to a local dealer there and then. Many saucepans and other items somehow got stolen as we ferried it through. Then eventually we were in and settled.

We had only been there for a few days when an old friend knocked on the door. It was Gary. I had led him to the Lord a couple of years earlier but had lost touch as he flitted in and out of the old drug lifestyle.

"How did you know I had moved here?" I asked him.

---

[12] 2 Samuel 24:24

"I spoke to Lurch, asking him if he knew your address as I had heard that you had moved back. He said that the only family that had moved in were born again Christians, into number 111."

"Blimey! News gets around," I answered.

Lurch was a notorious traveller drug dealer who lived at the other end of this huge street, at least one hundred houses away.

The impact we made came about without us having to do much at all. People just ended up knocking on our door. Still, life in the street was pretty much the same as I remembered, with my neighbours' windows being smashed in by an old friend who wanted to beat up the family living there; police cars taking people away; the local dialect of curse words being shouted out loud day and night. Strangely enough, though, we felt quite at home and secure for the first time in a house that we could call our own.

After we had been there for about one year, Sarah's brother turned up.

"I've just been to an auction with Big Ron, and guess what? Your old house was one of those auctioned today. I couldn't believe how cheap it went for. Some developer bought it for £70k. I just had to come round and tell you. That's some house for just seventy grand! If I had the money I would have bought it," he said.

I took some consolation that I had heard from God that the house would be sold for exactly £70k.

Although I now had a decent job and career path, plus church life was exciting, a deep dissatisfaction with the way things were grew in my heart. This was particularly true with my work. Although in my field I could be viewed as the most successful employee, bringing in more revenue than all my other colleagues put together, that was not the reason or passion I had gone there.

I remembered back to my final days at the sewerage farm, with how I had left that old boiler suit for a smart Savile Row suit. I had seen an advert in the local paper that seemed to describe me, and which then continued, "If you are like this, we would like to hear from you." The job entailed selling advertising space for a local reputable newspaper. The only suit I had was my wedding suit, but it was one of the best suits that money could buy – only because my stepdad at the time was a Savile Row tailor and it was his wedding present for me. I had gone and got measured up by the same tailors that Prince Charles, David Bowie and Edward Fox had used, to name just a few. I had chosen the cloth and style so that it was both smart and practical, not just fit for one day.

At the interview I had been very confident and felt smart. The Advertising Director who interviewed me was called Tim, and it was very apparent that he had recently had a hair transplant. His head looked like that of a doll, full of puncture holes with a single strand of hair poking out of each one. *Don't look at his head, don't look at his head,* I repeated to myself over and over.

He clearly liked me, then asked a direct question: "So then, Glenn, you look the part and I like you, but what makes you think you can sell advertising?"

"Well, Tim, as you saw on my CV, I am a Christian. I am experienced at sharing my faith, the Gospel, with all kinds of people, one to one, on the streets, in prisons, church and school. If I can be confident in this which people can't see, it should be easy for me to sell something that can be shown and explained," I answered.

Tim laughed. "I agree. You know, one of the best salesmen I have ever known personally was like you, a Christian."

Before I knew it, there I was, an office worker. In the beginning my colleagues were very weird with me, until one day one of them said, "You're OK. Actually, you're quite normal."

"Erm... thanks... I think!" I answered.

They then explained that they had all known that a 'born again' Christian was starting and expected a 'right weirdo'.

I had to laugh. "What, you all thought I'd be like the nun in the Blues Brothers and float about or something?" I asked.

Work became work, most of my colleagues became friends, and I did my job well and spoke freely about my faith. My story even made front page news when one of the reporters heard about my miraculous conversion. But now I was still the only Christian there; where were the salvations?

One winter's night I was driving to a senior leaders' meeting. (Although still in my twenties, I had been made a church leader.) It had only just stopped snowing and the roads were clear, so I was in good time. I was listening to a worship cassette and praying as I drove, when suddenly a deluge of snow dropped from the heavens bringing everything to a standstill. Although I enjoy driving in the snow and always welcome the challenge, for a few minutes I could not move. Then I once again heard God speak audibly, clearly and directly into my spirit: "You will see two major moves of my Spirit in this nation. Prepare for the second."

Wow! I thought. I understood what God was saying. We were to prepare for something that he was going to do, which would be so big that the only way to prepare would be to get our hearts right.

I sat there for a moment, then excitedly manoeuvred through the snow until I arrived at the meeting. I passionately shared what God had said to me, but no one else seemed that excited. I have now over the years heard the same prophecy from a variety of sources, and I believe that the second move of God will be revival, a season where God's Holy Spirit moves so powerfully that countless numbers of people get healed, saved, made whole and the name of Jesus is held once again in awe.[13]

A few weeks later, after an early morning prayer meeting and as I drove to work, I cried out to God, "Where are you, Lord? I've told them all about you at work; I've taken all the risks. When will you do what you are supposed to do? I know the timing may not be right, but at least give a taste of the good things to come! Give me a taster of revival, Lord, here and now!" I actually felt that I could not share my faith any more unless God turned up.

Things changed that very day. As I was photocopying documents, a colleague came up to me and asked, "Is it true only Christians go to heaven? And if so, tell me why."

People started seeking me out. The Holy Spirit began to move as God's kingdom invaded my place of work.

A manager of mine, Sue, had an unusual skin condition which affected the pigmentation on her arms.

"You believe God heals. Could you pray for me?" she asked.

To which I answered, "Yes, OK."

---

[13] An Old Testament prophet called Habakkuk prayed, "LORD, I have heard of your fame; I stand in awe of your deeds, Lord. Repeat them in our day, in our time make them known; in wrath remember mercy." (Habakkuk 3:2) As did the prophet Isaiah: "Oh, that you would rend the heavens and come down, that the mountains would tremble before you! As when fire sets twigs ablaze and causes water to boil, come down to make your name known to your enemies and cause the nations to quake before you! For when you did awesome things that we did not expect, you came down, and the mountains trembled before you. Since ancient times no one has heard, no ear has perceived, no eye has seen any God besides you, who acts on behalf of those who wait for him." (Isaiah 64:1-4)

Sue directed me to small office so we could have a bit of privacy. It was not much bigger than a broom cupboard. As we stood there alone, she asked what she should do. To be honest, I didn't have much of a clue but I made out that I did.

"Just stand there, close your eyes, put out your hand as though you are about to get a gift, and I'll pray," I instructed.

She complied, standing with her eyes shut and her hands open.

I stood behind her, eyes closed, raised one hand behind her back and asked God to heal her. Then I didn't know what else to say, so I started to pray in tongues.

Suddenly I became aware of something moving in front of me. It felt like a swinging pendulum, so I opened my eyes to peek. It was Sue; she was pivoting, swaying forwards and backwards, then in a single moment she collapsed on the floor as though dead. *Lord, you've killed her,* I thought in panic. Up until that time I had not seen anyone fall in the Spirit in this way, although later I saw God do this to many people, including me, in a lot of churches.

Another manager, Viv, tried to open the office door, so I quickly put my foot against it, so that she couldn't barge her way in. "What's going on in there?" she demanded.

"It's only me and Sue. We are having a one-to-one meeting, won't be long," I answered.

Viv once again tried to push the door open, but I refused to move my foot, wondering how to explain that I had just killed Sue.

Suddenly, Sue started to rise to her feet. She staggered and looked like a drunk. "It's OK, Viv. We're on our way out," she shouted.

Viv stared at us as we left that office, especially when Sue turned to me and said, "I did not even believe in God until then. Now I cannot deny he exists."

If ever I were to write a booklet on how to pray for someone, it would recommend quite the opposite of how I went about this.

On another occasion, when driving around with a colleague called Mike, I noticed that he kept rubbing his arm.

"You OK?" I asked him.

"No, I've got tennis elbow; it's killing me," he answered.

"Would you like to me to pray for you?" I suggested.

"OK," he replied.

I kept it simple this time, put one hand on his arm and said simply, "Lord, heal him."

Back at the office, Mike was moving his arm continually. "Hey, it's better," he said. "I've been healed."

The atmosphere was clearly different at work and then the conversions began.

One that sticks in my mind was with the first to convert, Pete. He was an annoying young man who worked in production. He would always ask the awkward questions. As usual, one morning he came over to me and said, "If God is real then what about..." and he went on to voice some objections.

I really could not be bothered to engage with him yet again, so I questioned him by saying, "Pete, if you died tonight, where do you think you would go?"

He went silent, then grew pale and asked, "Can I come to church with you this Sunday?"

He came along, responded to a salvation call, agreed to get baptised and was witnessing for Christ on Monday.

Donna is another example. She was a new sales rep whom I was to show around on her first day. As she got into my car she asked, "Are you a Christian?" to which I answered yes. She then said to me, "I used to be a Christian."

I said that there was no such thing as "used to be" and explained about God's grace. Within minutes she had rededicated her life to Christ and then went home and led her teenage son to Christ with her.

Then there was Tina. Tina hated me and everything that I stood for. Her best friend Angela shared a desk with me and I remember her saying, "If there is one person who would never convert, it would be Tina." Stupidly, forgetting who I once was, I agreed.

Then one Friday night, as a group of colleagues gathered around me to hear about the gospel, Tina was among them and said, "You are going to have the last laugh." I was dumbstruck; was she actually agreeing with me? Tina then got up and left the office. It wasn't long before one by one we left too.

On Sunday morning in church, there she was sitting in the service! Then, during a space for testimonies of God's goodness, she stood up at the front of the church and explained, "On Friday I did not believe in God, then yesterday while driving home from shopping, God's Spirit fell in my car and I understood for the first time." On Monday at work, Tina was witnessing powerfully for the Lord.

During those days of blessing, Tim had left the newspaper and been replaced by a lady director called Paula. She had made it very clear that she had problems with me and set out to give me a hard time. Within weeks of her arrival, she gathered the staff together, then called me to show them my wage slip for the month as she gave them out. I had worked very hard that month, surpassed all my targets and was financially rewarded.

"I want you all to know that Glenn has earned more money than me this month," she said in a way I assumed was to encourage her salespeople to keep going for it, but then she went dry and added, "You will never do that again!"

From that day on my targets soared, but somehow I always met them, although only just.

On a certain occasion the whole team was offered the incentive of a holiday in Paris for the one who would achieve the highest percentage rise in revenue for one particular month. Seeing that I was bringing in the highest revenue anyway, to get the highest percentage rise compared to others seemed unachievable – but I got it. Once the figures were confirmed, Paula came out and over to me.

"Glenn, did you get it in writing that you would go to Paris?"

"No," I answered.

"Well, you are not going, then," she said smugly.

My colleagues were furious. "What are you going to do about that?" they asked me.

"Nothing. First she tells me not to work too hard as there are no rewards for it, then she tells us all that her word stands for nothing and that we should not believe a word she says... I think she's done enough to herself, don't you?" I answered.

Everyone started laughing.

My friend Rob, who worked in the Telesales Department, was always asking questions about my faith, so one day I lent him a tape called 'Out of Darkness'. This tape was made by the Newfrontiers group of churches as an evangelistic giveaway tool. Three people told their personal stories – dramatic testimonies of what Jesus had done in their lives – and I was one of those people. As I drove to work the following day, I was listening to a copy of the tape and asked God to show me what he would say to Rob. I heard nothing until another story began in which a girl had been challenged by Jesus saying to her, "You either follow me or you don't." Those words seemed to ring in my ears.

I got to work before Rob, waiting excitedly for him to arrive. Then, as he walked over to me, I called out, "Hey, Rob, did you listen to the tape?"

"Yes, it was good," he replied sheepishly.

"Well, Rob..." I paused momentarily and then continued, "You either follow me or you don't."

Rob spun on his feet and looked like he was going to run out. Instead he stopped, walked over to me looking very pale and asked, "How did you know? How did you know that out of all that tape, the thing that really freaked me out was that?"

It's fun when we get in on what God is doing, an invite that goes out to all: "Come and play!"

One day, I had just returned from the office after turning a minor account into a major account, more than tripling the contracted agreement, when Paula heard and called me into her office. This time I really did expect a pat on the back. However, she stood there sombre-faced.

"If anyone else gets converted you are sacked," she said. "I forbid you to talk to my staff about Jesus."

"Really?" I replied, stunned.

"Yes! I forbid you from talking about Jesus during worktime," she demanded

"OK. What about after work and during lunch?" I enquired.

"No, no, no," she ranted. "I forbid you talking to anyone here about this Jesus. You must stop it, and I will sack you if you don't!" she demanded assertively.

I was further stunned by a picture of her that suddenly I saw in my spirit. In it she was sitting on a pile of rubble with the words "Your house is left to you desolate" written underneath.

I didn't know whether to tell her about this picture or what to with it, so I just said, "Paula, if you look back at my CV, it states that I'm a Christian. The fact that I like to share my faith is what landed me this position in the first place. To me, sharing my faith is like breathing and I will carry on. Oh – and by the way, there is another member of staff really interested in this gospel of salvation." (This other person was Paula's personal secretary, who seemed to be on the edge of committing her life to Christ.)

That was the end of our meeting, and I just walked out to carry on working.

Then, without any involvement from me, within just six weeks of this incident Paula was demoted to sitting opposite me each day and then made redundant. I wouldn't even try to explain the picture or what happened to Paula, except to say that God is holy and when he is doing an extraordinary thing, we must not stand against it.

I had been with the newspaper for over six years when I knew God had brought my time there to an end. Just before I left, I received a phone call from a colleague who had left a year prior to that – an enemy of the gospel and a member of the magic circle. He asked me how my walk with God was, which surprised me, but then he explained that he had since given his life to Christ and was attending a local church.

For a season it had been remarkably easy to win people for Christ. There were no formulas as to how that happened, and I believe it was just a taste of a revival that will one day, in my lifetime, come about in our nation.

I have lived through a move of God's Spirit that swept across nearly all denominations globally in the 1990s, but am still waiting and preparing for the second move that God promised me. The best is yet to come!

CHAPTER TWENTY-ONE

Freedom at Last

In Acts 14:22 we are told that "we must go through many hardships to enter the kingdom of God," and Jesus said in John 16:33, "I have told you these things so that in me you may have peace. In this world you will have trouble. But take heart! I have overcome the world." Jesus has guaranteed that even we who follow him will have many hardships and troubles. James the brother of Jesus said, "Consider it pure joy, my brothers and sisters, whenever you face trials of many kinds."[14]

After years of walking with Jesus, I was hit with a trial in which I could find no peace, let alone joy, to draw from. I felt deserted by God, only to find out that this wilderness experience was again set up to do me good. I now refer to those times as "being in the worst best place possible".

I was driving to work to set up for the evening youth session, totally exhausted mentally, physically and especially spiritually. The past five years of battling and enduring a torrent of severe challenges had taken its . toll. Suddenly, *bang!* I can only describe it as though my mind felt like it had exploded. I felt that I had no chance of landing. I screamed alone in my car for the whole journey, but somehow managed to continue functioning. By the end of the week, however, I could no longer cope at all and just gave up completely; I had at last come to the end of myself.

Even though I had walked with God, and had seen and experienced so much, so many successes and so many failures, my foundational walk was still dogged with fear and anxiety, and now what I feared most had come upon me. In this hopeless state, I feared the worst: that I would now lose control and become the monster I thought had been put to death. Fear tingled throughout my being.

---

[14] James 1:2

I asked Sarah to make me a doctor's appointment and to come with me. I could also not face work or any pressures at all. So we ended up entering the doctor's room and I sat opposite him.

"I need to be sectioned. Please lock me away!" was all I could say to him, as I feared that now that I had given up, demonic forces would take me over.

Fortunately, the surgery practice was a Christian one, so the doctors there were more spiritually intuitive than at secular surgeries. The doctor calmed me slightly and took my pulse. He was shocked at how high it was. After a few tests he prescribed tranquilisers, antidepressants and blood pressure tablets, as physically I was ready to burst. He also wondered whether I might have thyroid problems so booked further tests and arranged for me to come back in a couple of weeks. Then he sent me home.

Home... the place of safety. I loved my family dearly: Sarah my wife; Amy, Alice, Grace, Molly and Lydia, our five lovely daughters. We were yet to be blessed with our sixth daughter, Ellen. They were my treasures, but even my home was to become a place of torment.

It was at this point that the enemy of our souls really pressed in. Kick a man when he's down! I felt constantly anxious. Awake or sleeping, I could find no peace, and then the accusations started. I began to relive the condemnation of sin. I won't say 'conviction' of sin because when the Holy Spirit convicts us, he always leads us to repentance and freedom: "So then, even to Gentiles God has granted repentance that leads to life."[15] This was a barrage of condemnatory thoughts that pressed right through to the foundations of my faith.

"You put him in hospital. You did that. He nearly died and you didn't care one bit. You could have put him in hell, you cold-blooded, uncaring excuse of a human. How do you plead?" was the opening challenging voice to my soul.

"Guilty! I am guilty! I have no plead before me except guilt, but I plead the blood of Jesus over my life," I answered

Then I was challenged on and on. The fine details of my life before Jesus flashed before me.

Again and again I pleaded the same: "Guilty, but I plead the blood of Jesus over all my life."

---

[15] Acts 11:18

This went on day after day, night after night. I could not even leave my room; it became a prison of torment. Eventually the challenge moved deeper still.

"You plead the blood over your past life, but what about that supposed walk of faith. Look at the mistakes you've made, the failures you created."

"The blood of Jesus is my only plea, I cried on. I do not declare to have any righteousness of my own. I need my saviour today as much as when I first met him," I declared over every accusation.

Two weeks had nearly passed when the continual accusations mockingly moved to my then broken condition.

"Ha, man of faith? Look at you! You can't even face your own family. Locked in here with me, broken, anxious, a total failure at all you do. You can't even manage your life yet, so how could you be trusted to help other people? How do you plead now, oh faithless one?"

How my body and thoughts shook as I dug in deep for the only answer that I had.

"What answer can I give? I only have one! His blood, the blood of my saviour, Jesus. I am saved through the BLOOD. He has paid for my life in full. The precious blood of my saviour has paid for me! My past, my present and my future are all paid for by Jesus!" I declared.

Suddenly, after fifteen days of torment, all went silent and peaceful. Had the storm passed? I sat up, enjoying the stillness, but eventually broke the silence with a question of my own.

"Tormenter, have you anything else to accuse me with?" I called out.

"You will only answer with 'His blood, the blood of Jesus' so why should I?" came the answer

"That's the only answer I have and will ever have. In that case, I'm out of here!" I answered.

I got up and walked out of that room changed.

At the time of writing, seventeen years have passed since this moment that changed my foundational faith dramatically. Yes, I was saved the moment I cried out to Jesus in that school field nearly forty years ago, and since then I have been a work in progress and will be until I see him face to face, but I am being changed from one degree of glory to another, from freedom to freedom.

I'll close with one of my favourite promises, from Romans 8:38-39:

"For I am convinced that neither death nor life, neither angels nor demons, neither the present nor the future, nor any powers, neither height nor depth, nor anything else in all creation, will be able to separate us from the love of God that is in Christ Jesus our Lord."

Amen.

·

Epilogue

Since my initial crying out to God on that dreadful night and the writing of this book, nearly forty years of walking with Jesus have passed. Sarah and I now have six grown-up daughters and twelve grandchildren

The years have been full of challenges that have threatened to break us and miracles that have proved God's faithfulness. The many challenges that have hit us over years include two dramatic stories where two of our grandsons were miraculously healed after tragic and dramatic complications at birth – our first grandson was literally brought back from the dead.

I have also seen a braindead girl, whose very existence was just ebbing away in a hospital bed, be amazingly restored to full health after just one night of prayer, even though the medical staff were fully convinced that all hope was gone. On that occasion I audibly heard God say, "She will be fine. Pray for her."

I currently serve as the pastor of Vine Evangelical Church, Sevenoaks in Kent, England. With Sarah, I have helped plant churches and worked on national evangelistic strategies, as well as leading international missions. In our life of adventures we have moved home over twenty times – some moves a real blessing, but on most occasions leading to times of real anguish and hardships, all however in obedience to God's calling.

There have been times of going through wildernesses of the soul; others of being caught up in 'outpourings of God's Holy Spirit' with blessing and power. In short, we have so many stories to tell, it would take at least another book to share them. I believe that we have lived through the first wave of God's Spirit in our nation that he told me I would experience. Now I am waiting and watching for the second – a coming revival.

I hope that my story has brought you hope in whatever circumstance you may find yourself.

I have also grown in the revelation that God's grace is sufficient for me and the work that Jesus came to do is complete. I have also seen others to come to experience this personally for themselves in churches, restaurants, schools, prisons and on the streets – basically wherever this message of salvation has been shared.

My understanding of the gospel is simply this. Jesus lived a perfect life in total surrender to God his Father. He gave up that life by surrendering it to sinful men and was beaten, tortured and, after being totally abandoned, was crucified until dead upon a cross (also referred to as a tree). God's word says that "the wages of sin is death" and "cursed is anyone who is hung on a tree"[16].

Jesus had no sin yet still died. However, death had no charge or hold upon him, so he was raised to life on the third day. But still, he had faced and endured death, so a price had been paid; if his death did not pay for his own sin (for he had none), it can be for mine and yours. The death he died was for me, to pay my cost and yours.

I have accepted his death as my own. Whatever punishment I deserved, he went through and paid for in full because of his great love. He became the curse for me but now he is the great blessing of life.

He can be yours too. Would you dare pray what I once prayed over thirty-five years ago when I was about as lost as anyone could be? Whether you know him as your saviour or not, whatever you are facing or going through, however good or bad today may seem, I now invite you to pray this prayer with me:

"Jesus, you said that you would never turn anyone away who comes to you. You also said that everyone who calls on the name of the Lord will be saved! I can only come to you as I am, and I ask you now to come to me and show me what it means to truly know you. I humbly ask you to reveal to me all my wrongdoing (sin) and to help me turn away from it (repent). Show me who you are and how much you love me personally. Give me ears to hear your voice and a heart to understand. By the power of your Holy Spirit, bring me the revelation I need so that I can truly know you. Also, reassure me in your word that once I am yours, nothing can ever separate me from you and you will always be with me, from now and for all times. Amen."

---

[16] NKJV

What Shall I Read Next?

Outgrowing the Shackles
Helen Pollard
ISBN 978-1-78815-669-1

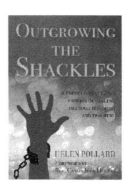

Emotional healing is often a process. God, in his infinite love and wisdom, addresses issues in our hearts in his own timing and not necessarily in the order we might choose. The freedom he brings us is not usually and instantaneous event, but a result of our growth and maturing as we allow him to gently touch every area of our lives.

God and Me in Three
Simon Flett
ISBN 978-1-907509-29-2

This book tells the stories of three years that changed the life of Simon Flett. Through his straight talk, lyrics and fascinating stories, he dares us to make the first step along the path he has followed.

Darkness to Destiny
Gwynneth Sunshine
ISBN 978-1-911086-67-3

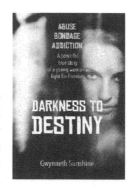

Gwynneth invested herself in spending time with, and praying for, the marginalised, but her efforts soon led to burnout, followed by a rapid downward spiral emotionally and spiritually. She began to encounter satanic activity, depression and sickness, along with abuse and rejection from those around her. Gradually she found herself drawn into the world of drug addiction, with poverty, suffering and violence. But she could not forget her childhood encounter with Jesus. In the midst of great darkness, she clung on to the hope of her destiny.